T0124603

IMMORTAL
YOUTH

IMMORTAL YOUTH

A Tribute to the Life and Station of the Báb

BAHÁ'Í
PUBLISHING

WILMETTE, ILLINOIS

Bahá'í Publishing
401 Greenleaf Avenue, Wilmette, Illinois 60091

Copyright © 2019 by the National Spiritual Assembly of the Bahá'ís of the United States

All rights reserved. Published 2019
Printed in the United States of America on acid-free paper ∞

22 21 20 19   4   3   2

ISBN 978-1-61851-149-2

Cover design by Carlos Esparza
Book design by Patrick Falso
Cover photo by Lindsey Lugsch-Tehle

Contents

Contents

Introduction

On the evening of 22 May 1844 a conversation took place in a private residence in the Persian city of Shíráz. Two figures spoke through the night and on into the dawn of the following day. It was a conversation destined to change the shape of history and reverberate through the ages and centuries to come. One man, Mullá Ḥusayn, was a spiritual seeker and traveler in search of the Promised Qá'im of Islam. His host, with whom he conversed, would prove to be the Object of his search. Siyyid 'Alí Muḥammad was a twenty-five-year-old merchant Who that night revealed Himself to be the Báb (meaning *the Gate* in Arabic), a Messenger of God, and the inaugurator of a new religious dispensation.

The Báb's announcement would lead to a dramatic shift in the Persian nation and in the world beyond. As soon as news of His message spread, thousands of people throughout the region rose up to align themselves with His Cause. At the same time, the government and the established clerical order, alarmed by the Báb's claims and the impact of His message, moved to crush the movement. What ensued was a series of waves of persecution and violent upheavals that played out on the streets of the towns and villages of Persia as the Báb's followers were attacked, tortured, and—in thousands of cases—mercilessly put to death for their unswerving devotion.

In July of 1850, just six years after declaring His station as a Manifestation of God, and having endured unrelenting persecution and harsh imprisonment, the Báb Himself was suspended by ropes in a town square in the city of Tabríz and executed by a firing squad of 750 soldiers. To many observers, the government's quest to snuff out the movement may have appeared successful. The Báb was gone and His followers were scattered and in disarray. His mission, however, was always destined to be short-lived and dramatic. While His station is that of an independent Manifestation of God and the Founder of a new religion, He was also the Herald of another. The Báb's purpose was to prepare the way for the coming of one He referred to as "He Whom God shall make manifest," the great world redeeming Figure alluded to in the prophecies of all of the world's great religions.

In 1863, Mírzá Ḥusayn-'Alí, known to us now as Bahá'u'lláh—having nurtured the Bábí community, reviving its spirits and deepening its knowledge while living as an exile in Baghdad—revealed Himself to be the Promised One to Whom the Báb referred. The appearance of These Twin Manifestations of God in the mid-nineteenth century and the significance of Their stations is something we can only dimly appreciate. In 2019, we now sit 200 years from the Báb's birth. The Bahá'í Faith, of which He is the Prophet-Herald, is an established independent religion with more than 5 million adherents worldwide. It is possibly the most ethnically and culturally diverse association of people on earth. Bahá'ís in virtually every corner of the world work to translate the Faith's vision of oneness and equality into a social reality.

Immortal Youth is not intended as a comprehensive or exhaustive compilation, but merely as a small commemorative volume collecting some of the sacred and authoritative texts of the Faith concerning the life and station of the Báb.

It contains writings of Bahá'u'lláh and the Báb, as well as writings and recorded utterances of 'Abdu'l-Bahá (the son and appointed successor of Bahá'u'lláh and the Head of the Bahá'í Faith from 1892 to 1921), and writings of Shoghi Effendi (the Guardian of the Faith from 1921 to 1957). The book is divided into sections covering the Báb's birth, declaration, martyrdom, and station, followed by a small selection of His prayers and meditations.

As we approach the bicentenary of the Báb's birth, just two years after that of the birth of Bahá'u'lláh, Bahá'ís the world over will gather once more in neighborhoods, villages, towns, and cities throughout the globe to commemorate and celebrate the occasion of the Twin Holy Days associated with the births of the Twin Manifestations of God for our age. It is hoped that this book will offer an opportunity for readers to reflect on the life and station of the inaugurator of the Bahá'í Dispensation, the towering Figure described by Bahá'u'lláh as "the Primal Point, the Divine Mystery, the Unseen Essence, the Dayspring of Divinity, and the Manifestation of Thy Lordship, through Whom all the knowledge of the past and all the knowledge of the future were made plain."[1]

Birth

Birch

1

In the name of the One born on this day,
Him Whom God hath made to be the Herald of His name,
the Almighty, the All-Loving!

This is a Tablet We have addressed unto that night wherein the heavens and the earth were illumined by a Light that cast its radiance over the entire creation.

Blessed art thou, O night! For through thee was born the Day of God, a Day which We have ordained to be the lamp of salvation unto the denizens of the cities of names, the chalice of victory unto the champions of the arenas of eternity, and the dawning-place of joy and exultation unto all creation.

Immeasurably exalted is God, the Maker of the heavens, Who hath caused this Day to speak forth that Name whereby the veils of idle fancy have been rent asunder, the mists of vain imaginings have been dispelled, and His name "the Self-Subsisting" hath dawned above the horizon of certitude. Through Thee the choice wine of everlasting life hath been unsealed, the doors of knowledge and utterance have been unlocked before the peoples of the earth, and the breezes of the All-Merciful have been wafted over every region. All glory be to that hour wherein the Treasure of God, the All-Powerful, the All-Knowing, the All-Wise, hath appeared!

O concourse of earth and heaven! This is that first night, which God hath made to be a sign of that second night, whereon was born He Whom no praise can befittingly extol and no attribute describe. Well is it with him who reflecteth upon them both: Verily, he will find their outer reality to correspond to their inner essence, and will become acquainted with the divine mysteries that lie enshrined in this Revelation, a Revelation through which the foundations of misbelief have been shaken, the idols of superstition have been shattered, and the banner hath been unfurled which proclaimeth, "No God is there but Him, the Powerful, the Exalted, the Incomparable, the Protector, the Mighty, the Inaccessible."

On this night the fragrance of nearness was wafted, the portals of reunion at the end of days were flung open, and all created things were moved to exclaim: "The Kingdom is God's, the Lord of all names, Who is come with world-embracing sovereignty!" On this night the Concourse on high celebrated the praise of their Lord, the Exalted, the Most Glorious, and the realities of the divine names extolled Him Who is the King of the beginning and the end in this Revelation, a Revelation through whose potency the mountains have hastened unto Him Who is the All-Sufficing, the Most High, and the hearts have turned towards the countenance of their Best-Beloved, and the leaves have been stirred into motion by the breezes of yearning, and the trees have raised their voices in joyful reply to the call of Him Who is the Unconstrained, and the entire earth hath trembled with longing in its desire to attain reunion with the Eternal King, and all things have been made new by that concealed Word which hath appeared in this mighty Name.

O night of the All-Bountiful! In thee do We verily behold the Mother Book. Is it a Book, in truth, or rather a child begotten? Nay, by Myself! Such words pertain to the realm of names, whilst God hath sanctified this Book above all names. Through it the Hidden Secret and the Treasured Mystery have been revealed. Nay, by My life! All that hath been mentioned pertaineth to the realm of attributes, whereas the Mother Book standeth supreme above this. Through it have appeared the manifestations of "There is no God but God" over them all. Nay, while such things have been proclaimed to all people, in the estimation of thy Lord naught but His ear is capable of hearing them. Blessed are those that are well assured!

Whereupon, dumbfounded, the Pen of the Most High cried out: "O Thou Who art exalted above all names! I adjure Thee by Thy might that encompasseth the heavens and the earth to exempt me from mentioning Thee, for I myself have been called into being by virtue of Thy creative power. How, then, can I depict that which all created things are powerless to describe? And yet, I swear by Thy glory, were I to proclaim that wherewith Thou hast inspired me, the entire creation would pass away from joy and ecstasy, how much more then would it be overwhelmed before the billows of the ocean of Thine utterance in this most luminous, most exalted and transcendent Spot! Absolve, O Lord, this faltering Pen from magnifying so august a station, and deal mercifully with me, O my Possessor and my King. Overlook then my trespasses in Thy presence. Thou, verily, art the Lord of bounty, the All-Powerful, the Ever-Forgiving, the Most Generous."

—Bahá'u'lláh

2

He is the Eternal, the One, the Single, the All-Possessing, the Most Exalted.

All praise be to Thee, O my God, inasmuch as Thou hast adorned the world with the splendour of the dawn following the night wherein was born the One Who heralded the Manifestation of Thy transcendent sovereignty, the Dayspring of Thy divine Essence and the Revelation of Thy supreme Lordship. I beseech Thee, O Creator of the heavens and Fashioner of names, to graciously aid those who have sheltered beneath the shadow of Thine abounding mercy and have raised their voices amidst the peoples of the world for the glorification of Thy Name.

O my God! Thou beholdest the Lord of all mankind confined in His Most Great Prison, calling aloud Thy Name, gazing upon Thy face, proclaiming that which hath enraptured the denizens of Thy kingdoms of revelation and of creation. O my God! I behold Mine own Self captive in the hands of Thy servants, yet the light of Thy sovereignty and the revelations of Thine invincible power shine resplendent from His face, enabling all to know of a certainty that Thou art God, and that there is none other God but Thee. Neither can the power of the powerful frustrate Thee, nor the ascendancy of the rulers prevail against Thee. Thou doest whatsoever Thou willest by virtue of Thy sovereignty which encompasseth all created things, and ordainest that which Thou pleasest through the potency of Thy behest which pervadeth the entire creation.

I implore Thee by the glory of Thy Manifestation and by the power of Thy might, Thy sovereignty and Thine exaltation to render victorious those who have arisen to serve Thee, who have aided Thy Cause and humbled themselves before the splendour of the light of Thy face. Make them then, O my God, triumphant over Thine enemies and cause them to be steadfast in Thy service, that through them the evidences of Thy dominion may be established throughout Thy realms and the tokens of Thine indomitable power be manifested in Thy lands. Verily Thou art potent to do what Thou willest; no God is there but Thee, the Help in Peril, the Self-Subsisting.

This glorious Tablet hath been revealed on the Anniversary of the Birth* that thou mayest recite it in a spirit of humility and supplication and give thanks unto thy Lord, the All-Knowing, the All-Informed. Make thou every effort to render service unto God, that from thee may appear that which will immortalize thy memory in His glorious and exalted heaven.

Say: Glorified art Thou, O my God! I implore Thee by the Dawning-Place of Thy signs and by the Revealer of Thy clear tokens to grant that I may, under all conditions, hold fast the cord of Thy loving providence and cling tenaciously to the hem of Thy generosity. Reckon me then with those whom the changes and chances of the world have failed to deter from serving Thee and from bearing allegiance unto Thee, whom the onslaught of the people hath been powerless to hinder from magnifying Thy Name and celebrating Thy praise. Graciously assist me, O my Lord, to do whatever Thou lovest and

---

* Of the Bab.

desirest. Enable me then to fulfil that which will exalt Thy Name and will set ablaze the fire of Thy love.

Thou art, in truth, the Forgiving, the Bountiful.*

—Bahá'u'lláh

---

* This selection, with the exception of the invocation, was first published in *Tablets of Bahá'u'lláh Revealed after the Kitáb-i-Aqdas*.

3

Through the revelation of Thy grace, O Lord, Thou didst call Me into being on a night such as this,* and lo, I am now lonely and forsaken in a mountain. Praise and thanksgiving be unto Thee for whatever conformeth to Thy pleasure within the empire of heaven and earth. And all sovereignty is Thine, extending beyond the uttermost range of the kingdoms of Revelation and Creation.

Thou didst create Me, O Lord, through Thy gracious favor and didst protect Me through Thy bounty in the darkness of the womb and didst nourish Me, through Thy loving-kindness, with life-giving blood. After having fashioned Me in a most comely form, through Thy tender providence, and having perfected My creation through Thine excellent handiwork and breathed Thy Spirit into My body through Thine infinite mercy and by the revelation of Thy transcendent unity, Thou didst cause Me to issue forth from the world of concealment into the visible world, naked, ignorant of all things, and powerless to achieve aught. Thou didst then nourish Me with refreshing milk and didst rear Me in the arms of My parents with manifest compassion, until Thou didst graciously acquaint Me with the realities of Thy Revelation and apprised

---

* Refers to the Báb's birthday on the first day of the month of Muharram, 1235 A.H. (October 20, 1819).

Me of the straight path of Thy Faith as set forth in Thy Book. And when I attained full maturity Thou didst cause Me to bear allegiance unto Thine inaccessible Remembrance, and enabled Me to advance towards the designated station, where Thou didst educate Me through the subtle operations of Thy handiwork and didst nurture Me in that land with Thy most gracious gifts. When that which had been preordained in Thy Book came to pass Thou didst cause Me, through Thy kindness, to reach Thy holy precincts and didst suffer Me, through Thy tender mercy, to dwell within the court of fellowship, until I discerned therein that which I witnessed of the clear tokens of Thy mercifulness, the compelling evidences of Thy oneness, the effulgent splendors of Thy majesty, the source of Thy supreme singleness, the heights of Thy transcendent sovereignty, the signs of Thy peerlessness, the manifestations of Thine exalted glory, the retreats of Thy sanctity, and whatsoever is inscrutable to all but Thee.

—The Báb

4

Thou art aware, O My God, that since the day Thou didst call Me into being out of the water of Thy love till I reached fifteen years of age I lived in the land which witnessed My birth [Shíráz]. Then Thou didst enable Me to go to the seaport [Búshihr] where for five years I was engaged in trading with the goodly gifts of Thy realm and was occupied in that with which Thou hast favored Me through the wondrous essence of Thy loving-kindness. I proceeded therefrom to the Holy Land [Karbilá] where I sojourned for one year. Then I returned to the place of My birth. There I experienced the revelation of Thy sublime bestowals and the evidences of Thy boundless grace. I yield Thee praise for all Thy goodly gifts and I render Thee thanksgiving for all Thy bounties. Then at the age of twenty-five I proceeded to thy sacred House [Mecca], and by the time I returned to the place where I was born, a year had elapsed. There I tarried patiently in the path of Thy love and beheld the evidences of Thy manifold bounties and of Thy loving-kindness until Thou didst ordain for Me to set out in Thy direction and to migrate to Thy presence. Thus I departed therefrom by Thy leave, spending six months in the land of Ṣád [Iṣfahán] and seven months in the First Mountain [Máh-kú], where Thou didst rain down upon Me that which beseemeth the glory of Thy heavenly blessings and befitteth the sublimity of Thy gracious gifts and favors. Now, in My thirtieth year, Thou beholdest Me, O My God, in this Grievous Mountain [Chihríq] where I have dwelt for one whole year.

Praise be unto Thee, O My Lord, for all times, heretofore and hereafter; and thanks be unto Thee, O My God, under all conditions, whether of the past or the future. The gifts Thou hast bestowed upon Me have reached their fullest measure and the blessings Thou hast vouchsafed unto Me have attained their consummation. Naught do I now witness but the manifold evidences of Thy grace and loving-kindness, Thy bounty and gracious favors, Thy generosity and loftiness, Thy sovereignty and might, Thy splendor and Thy glory, and that which befitteth the holy court of Thy transcendent dominion and majesty and beseemeth the glorious precincts of Thine eternity and exaltation.

—The Báb

5

The Báb was a young merchant of the Pure Lineage. He was born in the year one thousand two hundred and thirty-five [A.H.] on the first day of Muharram,* and when after a few years His father Siyyid Muḥammad-Riḍá died, He was brought up in Shíráz in the arms of His maternal uncle Mírzá Siyyid 'Alí the merchant. On attaining maturity He engaged in trade in Búshihr, first in partnership with His maternal uncle and afterwards independently. On account of what was observed in Him He was noted for godliness, devoutness, virtue, and piety, and was regarded in the sight of men as so characterized.

—'Abdu'l-Bahá

---

* 20 October 1819.

Declaration

Declaration

1

He is the All-Glorious.

This is the garden of Paradise, wherein arise the anthems of God, the Help in Peril, the Self-Subsisting; wherein ascend the soul-entrancing melodies warbled by the Nightingale of Eternity upon the twigs of the Divine Lote-Tree; wherein abide the Maids of Heaven whom none hath touched save God, the All-Glorious, the Most Holy; and wherein lieth enshrined that which draweth the needy to the shores of the ocean of true wealth and guideth the people to the Word of God. And this, verily, is naught but the manifest truth.

By Thy name "He"! Verily Thou art "He," O Thou Who art "He"!*

O Monk of the Divine Unity! Ring out the bell, for the Day of the Lord is come and the Beauty of the All-Glorious hath ascended His blessed and resplendent throne. Praise be to Thee, O Thou Who art "He," O Thou besides Whom there is none but "He"!

---

* In the Tafsír-i-Hú Bahá'u'lláh explains that the name "He" (or *Huva*, consisting of the letters Há' and Váv) is God's Most Great Name, for it is a mirror in which all of God's names and attributes are reflected together.

O Húd, Prophet of the Divine Decree! Sound the clarion in the name of God, the All-Glorious, the Most Bountiful, for the Temple of holiness hath been established upon the seat of supernal glory. Praise be to Thee, O Thou Who art "He," O Thou besides Whom there is none but "He"!

O Countenance of immortality! Pluck with the fingers of the spirit the sacred and wondrous strings, for the Beauty of the Divine Essence hath appeared, arrayed in a silken vesture of light. Praise be to Thee, O Thou Who art "He," O Thou besides Whom there is none but "He"!

O Angel of light! Sound a blast upon the trumpet at the advent of this Revelation, for the letter Há' hath been joined to the letter of ancient glory.* Praise be to Thee, O Thou Who art "He," O Thou besides Whom there is none but "He"!

O Nightingale of heaven! Warble upon the boughs of this celestial garden in the name of the Beloved, for the beauty of the Rose hath appeared from behind an impenetrable veil. Praise be to Thee, O Thou Who art "He," O Thou besides Whom there is none but "He"!

O Songster of Paradise! Trill out upon the twigs in these wondrous days, for God hath cast His effulgent rays upon all created things. Praise be to Thee, O Thou Who art "He," O Thou besides Whom there is none but "He"!

O Bird of eternity! Soar aloft in these heights, for the Bird of faithfulness hath soared in the atmosphere of divine nearness. Praise be to Thee, O Thou Who art "He," O Thou besides Whom there is none but "He"!

O denizens of Paradise! Sing out and chant in the sweetest of tones, for the melody of God hath been raised within the Tabernacle of matchless sanctity. Praise be to Thee, O Thou

---

* That is, the letter "B" in the name "Bahá."

Who art "He," O Thou besides Whom there is none but "He"!

O inmates of the Kingdom! Intone the name of the Beloved, for the beauty of His Cause hath shone forth from behind the veils, adorned with a luminous spirit. Praise be to Thee, O Thou Who art "He," O Thou besides Whom there is none but "He"!

O dwellers of the kingdom of names! Bedeck the furthest reaches of heaven, for the Most Great Name is come, riding upon the clouds of transcendent majesty. Praise be to Thee, O Thou Who art "He," O Thou besides Whom there is none but "He"!

O inhabitants of the Dominion of divine attributes in the Realm of Glory! Make ready to enter the presence of God, for the soft breezes of holiness have wafted from the sanctuary of the Divine Essence, and this, verily, is a conspicuous bounty. Praise be to Thee, O Thou Who art "He," O Thou besides Whom there is none but "He"!

O paradise of the Divine Unity! Rejoice within thyself, for the paradise of God, the Most Exalted, the All-Powerful, the All-Knowing, hath appeared. Praise be to Thee, O Thou Who art "He," O Thou besides Whom there is none but "He"!

O heaven of grandeur! Render thanks unto God within thine inmost being, for the heaven of holiness hath been upraised in the firmament of a heart of stainless purity. Praise be to Thee, O Thou Who art "He," O Thou besides Whom there is none but "He"!

O sun of worldly dominion! Eclipse thy face, for above the horizon of a resplendent morn there have shone the rays of the Day-Star of eternity. Praise be to Thee, O Thou Who art "He," O Thou besides Whom there is none but "He"!

O earth of knowledge! Swallow up thy learning, for the Earth of true knowledge hath been outspread through Him

Who is the Self of God, the All-Glorious, the All-Bountiful, the Most High. Praise be to Thee, O Thou Who art "He," O Thou besides Whom there is none but "He"!

O lamp of earthly sovereignty! Put out thy light, for the Lamp of God hath been lit within the niche of eternity and hath illumined all that are in heaven and all that are on earth. Praise be to Thee, O Thou Who art "He," O Thou besides Whom there is none but "He"!

O seas of the world! Still the pounding of your waves, for a most wondrous Cause hath made to surge the Crimson Sea. Praise be to Thee, O Thou Who art "He," O Thou besides Whom there is none but "He"!

O Peacock of the Divine Unity! Utter thy plaintive cry amidst the thickets of the celestial world, for the melody of God hath sounded near on every side. Praise be to Thee, O Thou Who art "He," O Thou besides Whom there is none but "He"!

O Cockerel of eternity! Sound thy call in the forests of the empyrean heaven, for the Summoner of God hath cried out from every lofty height. Praise be to Thee, O Thou Who art "He," O Thou besides Whom there is none but "He"!

O concourse of ardent lovers! Rejoice in your souls, for the day of separation hath ended, and the Covenant hath been fulfilled, and the Beloved hath appeared arrayed in sublime and majestic beauty. Praise be to Thee, O Thou Who art "He," O Thou besides Whom there is none but "He"!

O assemblage of mystic knowers! Let your hearts be filled with joy, for the time of remoteness hath passed, and the spirit of certitude hath appeared, and the countenance of the celestial Youth hath beamed forth, adorned with the ornament of holiness in the paradise of His name, the Almighty. Praise be to Thee, O Thou Who art "He," O Thou besides Whom there is none but "He"!

Glorified art Thou, O Lord, my God! I beseech Thee by Thy Day through which Thou didst bring forth all other days, and in a single moment whereof Thou didst reckon up the appointed time of all that have been and all that shall be— Praise be to Thee, O Thou Who art "He," O Thou besides Whom there is none but "He"!—

And by Thy Name which Thou hast made the sovereign of the kingdom of names and the ruler of all who are in heaven and all who are on earth—Praise be to Thee, O Thou Who art "He," O Thou besides Whom there is none but "He"!—

To graciously enable Thy servants to dispense with all but Thee, to draw nigh unto Thee, and to become detached from aught else save Thee. Thou, verily, art the God of power, of might and mercy. Praise be to Thee, O Thou Who art "He," O Thou besides Whom there is none but "He"!

Enable them then, O my God, to bear witness to Thy unity and to testify to Thy oneness in such wise that they may behold naught save Thee and shut their eyes to all else. Thou, in truth, art powerful to do what pleaseth Thee. Praise be to Thee, O Thou Who art "He," O Thou besides Whom there is none but "He"!

Kindle, then, within their breasts, O my Beloved, the fire of Thy love, that it may burn away the mention of aught else, and that they may testify within themselves that from everlasting Thou hast dwelt within the inaccessible heights of Thine eternity, that Thou wert alone with none beside Thee, and that Thou wilt continue unto everlasting to be what Thou hast ever been. No God is there but Thee, the Lord of might and bounty. Praise be to Thee, O Thou Who art "He," O Thou besides Whom there is none but "He"!

For were Thy servants who long to scale the heights of Thy unity to set their hearts upon aught except Thee, they could not be reckoned among such as have truly believed, nor would the sign of Thy singleness be found within them. Praise be to Thee, O Thou Who art "He," O Thou besides Whom there is none but "He"!

Glorified art Thou, O Lord my God! Such being the case, I implore Thee to send down from the clouds of Thy mercy that which shall purify the hearts of Thine ardent lovers and sanctify the souls of those who adore Thee. Raise them up, then, through Thy transcendent power, and render them victorious over all who dwell on earth. This, indeed, is that which Thou hast promised Thy loved ones through Thy word of truth: "And We desire to show favour to those who were brought low in the land, and to make them spiritual leaders among men, and to make of them Our heirs."* Praise be to Thee, O Thou Who art "He," O Thou besides Whom there is none but "He"!

—Bahá'u'lláh

* Qur'án 28:5.

2

*This is a remembrance of that which was revealed in the year
sixty in the days of God, the Almighty, the Help in Peril, the
All-Glorious, the All-Knowing.*

Lo, the gates of Paradise were unlocked, and the hallowed
Youth came forth bearing a serpent plain.* Rejoice! This is
the immortal Youth, come with crystal waters.

Upon His face was a veil woven by the fingers of might
and power. Rejoice! This is the immortal Youth, come with a
mighty name.

Upon His brow there shone a beauteous crown, which
cast its splendour upon all who are in heaven and all who are
on earth. Rejoice! This is the immortal Youth, come with a
mighty cause.

Upon His shoulders there fell the locks of the spirit, like
unto black musk upon white and lustrous pearls. Rejoice!
This is the immortal Youth, come with a transcendent cause.

On His right hand was a ring adorned with a pure and
blessed gem. Rejoice! This is the immortal Youth, come with
a mighty spirit.

Upon it was graven, in a secret and ancient script: "By God!
A most noble Angel is this."** And the hearts of the inmates

---

* See Qur'án 7:107.
** Cf. Qur'án 12:31.

of the eternal realm cried out: "Rejoice! This is the immortal Youth, come with an ancient light."

Upon His right cheek was a mark whose sight caused every man of understanding to waver in his faith. And they that dwell behind the veil of the Unseen exclaimed: "Rejoice! This is the immortal Youth, come with a mighty secret."

This is the Point from which the knowledge of the former and the latter generations hath been unfolded. And the denizens of the Kingdom intoned: "Rejoice! This is the immortal Youth, come with a mighty knowledge."

This, verily, is the Horseman of the Spirit Who circleth round the fount of everlasting life. And they that lie concealed in the retreats of the highest heaven cried out: "Rejoice! This is the immortal Youth, come with a mighty unveiling."

He descended from the tabernacle of beauty till He stood, even as the sun in the midmost heaven, arrayed with a beauty at once peerless and transcendent. Rejoice! This is the immortal Youth, come with the most joyful tidings!

Standing in the midmost heaven, He shone forth like unto the sun in its meridian splendour, illumining the seat of divine beauty with His mighty Name. Whereupon the Crier cried out: "Rejoice! This is the Beauty of the Unseen, come with a mighty spirit."

And the Maids of Heaven cried out from their celestial chambers: "Hallowed be the Lord, the most excellent of all creators!" And the nightingale sang sweetly: "Rejoice! This is the immortal Youth, Whose like the eyes of the favoured ones of Heaven have never beheld."

And lo, the gates of Paradise were unlocked a second time with the key of His Great Name. "Rejoice! This is the immortal Youth, come with a mighty name."

And the Maid of beauty shone forth even as the dawning sun above the horizon of a resplendent morn. Rejoice! This is the divine Maiden, come with surpassing beauty.

She came forth with such adorning as to seize with longing desire the minds of them that are nigh unto God. Rejoice! This is the Maid of Heaven, come with alluring charm.

Descending from the chambers of eternity, she sang in accents that entranced the souls of the sincere. Rejoice! This is the immortal Beauty, come with a mighty secret.

Suspended in the air, she let fall a single lock of her hair from beneath her luminous veil—Rejoice! This is the Maid of Heaven, come with a wondrous spirit—

Shedding the fragrance of that lock upon all creation. Whereupon the faces of the holy ones grew pale and the hearts of the ardent lovers were filled with the blood of anguish. Rejoice! This is the Maid of Heaven, come with the sweetest fragrance.

By God! Whosoever closeth his eyes to her beauty hath fallen prey to grave deception and manifest error. Rejoice! This is the immortal Beauty, come with a shining light.

She turned, and round her circled the inhabitants of both this world and the world to come. Rejoice! This is the Maid of Heaven, come with a mighty dispensation.

She advanced, arrayed with a rare and glorious adorning, till she stood face to face before the Youth. Rejoice! This is the immortal Beauty, come with enchanting grace.

From beneath her veil she drew forth her hand, golden tinged as a sunbeam falling upon the face of a stainless mirror. Rejoice! This is the immortal Beauty, come with a resplendent adorning.

Her incomparable ruby fingers seized the hem of the veil that hid the face of the Youth—Rejoice! This is the immortal Beauty, come with a mighty glance—

And drew it back, whereupon the pillars of the Throne on high were made to tremble. Rejoice! This is the immortal Youth, come with a mighty cause.

Then did the spirits of all created things part from their bodies. Rejoice! This is the immortal Youth, come with a mighty cause.

And the inmates of Paradise rent their garments asunder as they caught a lightning glimpse of His ancient and shining countenance. Rejoice! This is the immortal Youth, come with an effulgent light.

At that moment the Voice of the Eternal was heard from beyond the veil of clouds with a sweet and enchanting call. Rejoice! This is the immortal Youth, come with a mighty enchantment.

And from the source of God's inscrutable decree the Tongue of the Unseen proclaimed: "By God! The like of this Youth the eyes of the former generations have never beheld." Rejoice! This is the immortal Youth, come with a mighty cause.

And the maids of holiness cried out from the chambers of exalted dominion. Rejoice! This is the immortal Youth, come with manifest sovereignty.

By God! This is that Youth Whose beauty is the ardent desire of the celestial Concourse. Rejoice! This is the immortal Youth, come with a mighty cause.

Then did the Youth lift up His head to the concourse of heavenly angels—Rejoice! This is the immortal Youth, come with a mighty spirit—

And gave voice to a single word, whereupon the denizens of heaven arose, one and all, to a new life. Rejoice! This is the immortal Youth, come with a mighty trumpet blast.

He looked then upon the inhabitants of the earth with a wondrous glance. Rejoice! This is the immortal Youth, come with a mighty glance.

And with that glance He gathered them together each and all. Rejoice! This is the immortal Youth, come with a mighty cause.

With another look He signalled to a chosen few, then repaired to His habitation in the everlasting Paradise. And this, truly, is a mighty cause!

The Herald of Eternity proclaimeth from his cloud-wrapped throne: O ye that wait expectant in the vale of patience and fidelity! O ye that long to soar in the atmosphere of nearness and reunion! The celestial Youth, hidden ere now within the inviolable treasuries of God, hath appeared, even as the Sun of Reality and the Eternal Spirit, from the Dawning-Place of changeless splendour, adorned with the ornament of the Almighty and the beauty of the All-Praised. He hath rescued all who are in heaven and on earth from the perils of death and extinction, clothed them in the garment of true and ever-lasting existence, and bestowed upon them a new life.

That concealed Word upon which the souls of all the Messengers of God and His Chosen Ones have ever depended hath manifested itself out of the invisible world into the visible plane. No sooner had this hidden Word shone forth from the Realm of inmost being and absolute singleness to illumine the peoples of the earth than a breeze of mercy wafted therefrom, purifying all things from the stench of sin and arraying the countless forms of existence and the reality of man with the vesture of forgiveness. So great was the wondrous grace which pervaded all things that through the utterance of the letters 'B" and "E" the gems that lay hid within the repositories of this contingent world were brought forth and made manifest. Thus were the seen and the unseen joined in one garment, and the hidden and the manifest clothed in a single robe; thus did utter nothingness attain the realm of eternity, and pure evanescence gain admittance into the court of everlasting life.

Wherefore, O ye lovers of the beauty of the All-Glorious! O ye that ardently seek the court of the presence of the Almighty! This is the day of nearness and reunion, not the time for contention and idle words. If ye be sincere lovers, behold the beauty of the Best-Beloved shining clear and resplendent as the true morn. It behoveth you to be free from all attachment, whether to yourselves or to others; nay, ye should renounce existence and non-existence, light and darkness, glory and abasement alike. Sever your hearts from all transitory things, from all idle fancies and vain imaginings, that ye may, pure and unsullied, enter the realm of the spirit and partake with radiant hearts of the splendours of everlasting holiness.

O friends! The wine of eternal life is flowing. O lovers! The face of the Beloved is unveiled and unconcealed. O companions! The fire of the Sinai of love is burning bright and resplendent. Cast off the burden of love for this world and every attachment thereto, and, even as luminous, heavenly birds, soar in the atmosphere of the celestial Paradise and wing your flight to the everlasting nest. For devoid of this, life itself hath no worth, and bereft of the Beloved, the heart is of no account.

Yea, the moth-like lovers of the All-Glorious at every instant offer up their lives round the consuming flame of the Friend, occupying themselves with naught save Him. Yet not every bird can aspire to such heights. God, verily, guideth whom He willeth unto His mighty and exalted path.

Thus do We bestow upon the dwellers of the mystic realm that which shall draw them nigh unto the right hand of everlasting life and enable them to attain unto that station which hath been upraised in the heaven of holiness.

—Bahá'u'lláh

3

He is the Ever-Abiding, the Most Exalted, the Most Great.

Lo, the Tongue of Glory hath called aloud and the Word of God hath cried out, proclaiming: "The Kingdom is God's, the Creator of the heavens and the Lord of all names!" And yet the people, for the most part, are heedless. The entire creation resoundeth with the melodies of the All-Merciful, the realms of sanctity are redolent with the fragrance of His raiment, and the Most Great Name hath shed the splendour of His glory upon all who dwell on earth, and yet the people are wrapped in a palpable veil.

O Pen of Glory! Intone the anthems of grandeur, for We have inhaled the fragrance of reunion at the approach of that Day whereon the kingdom of names was adorned with the ornament of Our Name, the Exalted, the Most High. No sooner was this Day mentioned before the Throne than the Maids of Heaven chanted a wondrous melody, the Nightingale pealed out its heavenly song, and the All-Merciful gave voice to that which enraptured the souls of the Messengers of God, His chosen ones, and those who enjoy near access to Him.

This is the eve of that Day from whose horizon the ancient Morn hath dawned forth with the splendour of the light beaming from that effulgent horizon. Say: This is the Day whereon God established the Covenant concerning Him Who is the voice of Truth* by sending forth the One** Who imparted unto humankind the glad-tidings of this Great Announcement. This is the Day whereon the Most Great Sign appeared and proclaimed this mighty Name, captivating thereby all created things with the reviving breezes of the verses of God. Happy the one that hath recognized his Lord and is numbered with them that have attained His presence.

Say: He, verily, is the most perfect Balance established amongst the nations, through Whom the measures of all things are made manifest by Him Who is the All-Knowing, the All-Wise. He it is Who hath intoxicated every understanding heart with the wine of His utterance, and Who hath torn asunder the veils through the power of My Name that overshadoweth the worlds. He, verily, hath ordained the Bayán to be a leaf of this Garden and adorned it with the mention of this incomparable Remembrance. He hath admonished all men not to withhold themselves from the Dayspring of ancient glory, nor to cling, at the time of His manifestation, to such tales and traditions as are current amongst them. Thus hath it been decreed in accordance with that which He hath revealed, and unto this beareth witness He Who speaketh the truth. No God is there beside Me, the Almighty, the Most Generous.

They that have turned away from the latter Manifestation have indeed failed to recognize the former. Thus hath it been ordained by the Author of all causes in this mighty adornment. Say: He, verily, announced unto you this Root; wherefore they that are held back by reason of a mere branch

---

* Bahá'u'lláh.
** The Báb.

are in truth accounted among the dead. Alas, the people are clinging to the branch and have turned away from God, the King, the Glorious, the All-Praised. He conditioned all that He hath revealed upon Mine acceptance and made every matter contingent upon this manifest and resistless Cause. But for Me, He would not have uttered a single word, nor would He have manifested Himself before all who are in heaven and on earth. How often did He lament My banishment, My captivity, and My tribulations! That which was sent down in the Bayán beareth witness unto this, could ye but perceive it. Powerful indeed is the one who, through the might of God, hath become severed from all else but Him, and powerless the one who hath turned away from Him after He hath appeared with manifest sovereignty.

O peoples of the earth! Make mention of God on this Day whereon the Spirit hath spoken and the realities of those who were created by the Word of God, the Mighty, the Exalted, have ascended unto Him. It behoveth everyone on this day to rejoice with exceeding gladness, to clothe himself in his finest attire, to celebrate the praise of his Lord, and to give thanks unto Him for this most great favour. Blessed are they that have apprehended the purpose of God, and woe betide the heedless.

Having revealed this Tablet on this night, We desire to send it unto thee as a token of Our grace, that thou mayest be of those who are grateful. After thou hast received it, recite it in the presence of the loved ones of God, that they may hearken unto that which the Tongue of Grandeur hath pronounced and be of those who act in accordance with its counsels. Thus have We singled thee out and adorned thee with that raiment wherewith We have adorned the pure in heart. Praise be to God, the Lord of the worlds!

—Bahá'u'lláh

4

This is 23 May, the anniversary of the message and Declaration of the Báb. It is a blessed day and the dawn of manifestation, for the appearance of the Báb was the early light of the true morn, whereas the manifestation of the Blessed Beauty, Bahá'u'lláh, was the shining forth of the sun. Therefore, it is a blessed day, the inception of the heavenly bounty, the beginning of the divine effulgence. On this day in 1844 the Báb was sent forth heralding and proclaiming the Kingdom of God, announcing the glad tidings of the coming of Bahá'u'lláh and withstanding the opposition of the whole Persian nation. Some of the Persians followed Him. For this they suffered the most grievous difficulties and severe ordeals. They withstood the tests with wonderful power and sublime heroism. Thousands were cast into prison, punished, persecuted and martyred. Their homes were pillaged and destroyed, their possessions confiscated. They sacrificed their lives most willingly and remained unshaken in their faith to the very end. Those wonderful souls are the lamps of God, the stars of sanctity shining gloriously from the eternal horizon of the will of God.

The Báb was subjected to bitter persecution in Shíráz, where He first proclaimed His mission and message. A period of famine afflicted that region, and the Báb journeyed to Iṣfahán. There the learned men rose against Him in great hostility. He was arrested and sent to Tabríz. From thence He was transferred to Mákú and finally imprisoned in the strong castle of Chihríq. Afterward He was martyred in Tabríz.

This is merely an outline of the history of the Báb. He withstood all persecutions and bore every suffering and ordeal with unflinching strength. The more His enemies endeavored to extinguish that flame, the brighter it became. Day by day His Cause spread and strengthened. During the time when He was among the people He was constantly heralding the coming of Bahá'u'lláh. In all His Books and Tablets He mentioned Bahá'u'lláh and announced the glad tidings of His manifestation, prophesying that He would reveal Himself in the ninth year. He said that in the ninth year "you will attain to all happiness"; in the ninth year "you will be blessed with the meeting of the Promised One of Whom I have spoken." He mentioned the Blessed Perfection, Bahá'u'lláh, by the title "Him Whom God shall make manifest." In brief, that blessed Soul offered His very life in the pathway of Bahá'u'lláh, even as it is recorded in historical writings and records. In His first Book, the Best of Stories, He says, "O Remnant of God! I am wholly sacrificed to Thee; I am content with curses in Thy path; I crave nought but to be slain in Thy love; and God, the Supreme, sufficeth as an eternal protection."

Consider how the Báb endured difficulties and tribulations; how He gave His life in the Cause of God; how He was attracted to the love of the Blessed Beauty, Bahá'u'lláh; and how He announced the glad tidings of His manifestation. We must follow His heavenly example; we must be self-sacrificing and aglow with the fire of the love of God. We must partake of the bounty and grace of the Lord, for the Báb has admonished us to arise in service to the Cause of God, to be absolutely severed from all else save God during the day of the Blessed Perfection, Bahá'u'lláh, to be completely attracted by the love of Bahá'u'lláh, to love all humanity for His sake, to be lenient and merciful to all for Him and to upbuild the oneness of the world of humanity. Therefore, this day, 23 May, is the anniversary of a blessed event.

—'Abdu'l-Bahá

5

As for the Báb*—may my soul be His sacrifice!—it was at a young age, that is, in the twenty-fifth year of His blessed life, that He arose to proclaim His Cause. Among the Shí'ihs it is universally acknowledged that He never studied in any school, nor acquired learning from any teacher. To this the people of Shíráz, each and all, bear witness. Nevertheless, He suddenly appeared before the people, endowed with consummate knowledge, and though but a merchant, confounded all the divines of Persia. Alone, He undertook a task that can scarcely be conceived, for the Persians are known throughout the world for their religious fanaticism. This illustrious Being arose with such power as to shake the foundations of the religious laws, customs, manners, morals, and habits of Persia, and instituted a new law, faith, and religion. Though the eminent men of the State, the majority of the people, and the leaders of religion arose one and all to destroy and annihilate Him, He single-handedly withstood them and set all of Persia in motion. How numerous the divines, the leaders, and the inhabitants of that land who with perfect joy and gladness offered up their lives in His path and hastened to the field of martyrdom!

---

* 'Abdu'l-Bahá refers to the Báb by His title Ḥaḍrat-i-A'lá—His Holiness the Exalted One—but He will be designated here by the name under which He is known in the West.

The government, the nation, the clergy, and prominent leaders sought to extinguish His light, but to no avail. At last His moon rose, His star shone forth, His foundation was secured, and His horizon was flooded with light. He trained a large multitude through divine education and exerted a marvellous influence upon the thoughts, customs, morals, and manners of the Persians. He proclaimed the glad-tidings of the manifestation of the Sun of Bahá to all His followers and readied them for faith and certitude.

The manifestation of such marvellous signs and mighty undertakings, the influence exerted upon the thoughts and minds of the people, the laying of the foundations of progress, and the establishment of the prerequisites of success and prosperity by a young merchant constitute the greatest proof that He was a universal Educator—a fact that no fair-minded person would ever hesitate to acknowledge.

—'Abdu'l-Bahá

6

The opening scene of the initial act of this great drama was laid in the upper chamber of the modest residence of the son of a mercer of <u>Sh</u>íráz, in an obscure corner of that city. The time was the hour before sunset, on the 22nd day of May, 1844. The participants were the Báb, a twenty-five year old siyyid, of pure and holy lineage, and the young Mullá Ḥusayn, the first to believe in Him. Their meeting immediately before that interview seemed to be purely fortuitous. The interview itself was protracted till the hour of dawn. The Host remained closeted alone with His guest, nor was the sleeping city remotely aware of the import of the conversation they held with each other. No record has passed to posterity of that unique night save the fragmentary but highly illuminating account that fell from the lips of Mullá Ḥusayn.

"I sat spellbound by His utterance, oblivious of time and of those who awaited me," he himself has testified, after describing the nature of the questions he had put to his Host and the conclusive replies he had received from Him, replies which had established beyond the shadow of a doubt the validity of His claim to be the promised Qá'im. "Suddenly the call of the Mu'a<u>dhdh</u>in, summoning the faithful to their morning prayer, awakened me from the state of ecstasy into which I seemed to have fallen. All the delights, all the ineffable glories, which the Almighty has recounted in His Book as the priceless possessions of the people of Paradise—these I seemed to be experiencing that night. Methinks I was in a place of which it could be truly said: '*Therein no toil shall reach us, and therein no weariness shall touch us;*' '*no vain discourse shall they hear therein, nor any falsehood, but only the cry, "Peace! Peace!"*'; '*their cry therein shall be, "Glory be to Thee, O God!" and their salutation therein, "Peace!"*', and the close of their cry, "*Praise be to God, Lord of all creatures!*" 'Sleep had departed from me that night. I was enthralled by the music of that voice which rose and fell as He chanted; now swelling forth as He revealed verses of the Qayyúmu'l-Asmá', again acquiring ethereal, subtle harmonies as He uttered the prayers He was revealing. At the end of each invocation, He would repeat this verse: '*Far from the glory of thy Lord, the All-Glorious, be that which His creatures affirm of Him! And peace be upon His Messengers! And praise be to God, the Lord of all beings!*'"

"This Revelation," Mullá Ḥusayn has further testified, "so suddenly and impetuously thrust upon me, came as a thunderbolt which, for a time, seemed to have benumbed my faculties. I was blinded by its dazzling splendor and overwhelmed by its crushing force. Excitement, joy, awe, and wonder stirred the depths of my soul. Predominant among these emotions was a sense of gladness and strength which seemed to have transfigured me. How feeble and impotent, how dejected and timid, I had felt previously! Then I could neither write nor walk, so tremulous were my hands and feet. Now, however, the knowledge of His Revelation had galvanized my being. I felt possessed of such courage and power that were the world, all its peoples and its potentates, to rise against me, I would, alone and undaunted, withstand their onslaught. The universe seemed but a handful of dust in my grasp. I seemed to be the voice of Gabriel personified, calling unto all mankind: 'Awake, for, lo! the morning Light has broken. Arise, for His Cause is made manifest. The portal of His grace is open wide;

enter therein, O peoples of the world! For He Who is your promised One is come!'"

A more significant light, however, is shed on this episode, marking the Declaration of the Mission of the Báb, by the perusal of that *"first, greatest and mightiest"* of all books in the Bábí Dispensation, the celebrated commentary on the Súrih of Joseph, the first chapter of which, we are assured, proceeded, in its entirety, in the course of that night of nights from the pen of its divine Revealer. The description of this episode by Mullá Ḥusayn, as well as the opening pages of that Book attest the magnitude and force of that weighty Declaration. A claim to be no less than the mouthpiece of God Himself, promised by the Prophets of bygone ages; the assertion that He was, at the same time, the Herald of One immeasurably greater than Himself; the summons which He trumpeted forth to the kings and princes of the earth; the dire warnings directed to the Chief Magistrate of the realm, Muḥammad S̲h̲áh; the counsel imparted to Ḥájí Mírzá Áqásí to fear God, and the peremptory command to abdicate his authority as grand vizir of the S̲h̲áh and submit to the One Who is the *"Inheritor of the earth and all that is therein";* the challenge issued to the rulers of the world proclaiming the self-sufficiency of His Cause, denouncing the vanity of their ephemeral power, and calling upon them to *"lay aside, one and all, their dominion,"* and deliver His Message to *"lands in both the East and the West"*—these constitute the dominant features of that initial contact that marked the birth, and fixed the date, of the inception of the most glorious era in the spiritual life of mankind.

With this historic Declaration the dawn of an Age that signalizes the consummation of all ages had broken.

—Shoghi Effendi

Martyrdom

Martyrdom

1

Give ear, O My servant, unto that which is being sent down unto thee from the Throne of thy Lord, the Inaccessible, the Most Great. There is none other God but Him. He hath called into being His creatures, that they may know Him, Who is the Compassionate, the All-Merciful. Unto the cities of all nations He hath sent His Messengers, Whom He hath commissioned to announce unto men tidings of the Paradise of His good-pleasure, and to draw them nigh unto the Haven of abiding security, the Seat of eternal holiness and transcendent glory.

Some were guided by the Light of God, gained admittance into the court of His presence, and quaffed, from the hand of resignation, the waters of everlasting life, and were accounted of them that have truly recognized and believed in Him. Others rebelled against Him, and rejected the signs of God, the Most Powerful, the Almighty, the All-Wise.

Ages rolled away, until they attained their consummation in this, the Lord of days, the Day whereon the Day-Star of the Bayán manifested itself above the horizon of mercy, the Day in which the Beauty of the All-Glorious shone forth in the exalted person of 'Alí-Muḥammad, the Báb. No sooner did He reveal Himself, than all the people rose up against Him. By some He was denounced as one that hath uttered slanders against God, the Almighty, the Ancient of Days. Others regarded Him as a man smitten with madness, an allegation which I, Myself, have heard from the lips of one of the divines. Still others disputed His claim to be the Mouthpiece of God, and stigmatized Him as one who had stolen and used as his the words of the Almighty, who had perverted their meaning, and mingled them with his own. The Eye of Grandeur weepeth sore for the things which their mouths have uttered, while they continue to rejoice upon their seats.

"God," said He, "is My witness, O people! I am come to you with a Revelation from the Lord, your God, the Lord of your fathers of old. Look not, O people, at the things ye possess. Look rather at the things God hath sent down unto you. This, surely, will be better for you than the whole of creation, could ye but perceive it. Repeat the gaze, O people, and consider the testimony of God and His proof which are in your possession, and compare them unto the Revelation sent down unto you in this Day, that the truth, the infallible truth, may be indubitably manifested unto you. Follow not, O people, the steps of the Evil One; follow ye the Faith of the All-Merciful, and be ye of them that truly believe. What would it profit man, if he were to fail to recognize the Revelation of God? Nothing whatever. To this Mine own Self, the Omnipotent, the Omniscient, the All-Wise, will testify."

The more He exhorted them, the fiercer grew their enmity, till, at the last, they put Him to death with shameful cruelty. The curse of God be upon the oppressors!

A few believed in Him; few of Our servants are the thankful. These He admonished, in all His Tablets—nay, in every passage of His wondrous writings—not to give themselves up in the Day of the promised Revelation to anything whatever, be it in the heaven or in the earth. "O people!" said He, "I have revealed Myself for His Manifestation, and have caused My Book, the Bayán, to descend upon you for no other purpose except to establish the truth of His Cause. Fear ye God, and contend not with Him as the people of the Qur'án have contended with Me. At whatever time ye hear of Him, hasten ye towards Him, and cleave ye to whatsoever He may reveal unto you. Naught else besides Him can ever profit you, no, not though ye produce from first to last the testimonies of all those who were before you."

And when after the lapse of a few years the heaven of Divine decree was cleft asunder, and the Beauty of the Báb appeared in the clouds of the names of God, arrayed in a new raiment, these same people maliciously rose up against Him, Whose light embraceth all created things. They broke His Covenant, rejected His truth, contended with Him, cavilled at His signs, treated His testimony as falsehood, and joined the company of the infidels. Eventually, they determined to take away His life. Such is the state of them who are in a far-gone error!

And when they realized their powerlessness to achieve their purpose, they arose to plot against Him. Witness how every moment they devise a fresh device to harm Him, that they may injure and dishonour the Cause of God. Say: Woe be to you! By God! Your schemings cover you with shame. Your Lord, the God of mercy, can well dispense with all creatures. Nothing whatever can either increase or diminish the things He doth possess. If ye believe, to your own behoof will ye believe; and if ye believe not, ye yourselves will suffer. At no time can the hand of the infidel profane the hem of His Robe.

O My servant that believest in God! By the righteousness of the Almighty! Were I to recount to thee the tale of the things that have befallen Me, the souls and minds of men would be incapable of sustaining its weight. God Himself beareth Me witness. Watch over thyself, and follow not the footsteps of these people. Meditate diligently upon the Cause of thy Lord.

Strive to know Him through His own Self and not through others. For no one else besides Him can ever profit thee. To this all created things will testify, couldst thou but perceive it.

Emerge from behind the veil, by the leave of thy Lord, the All-Glorious, the Most Powerful, and seize, before the eyes of those who are in the heavens and those who are on the earth, the Chalice of Immortality, in the name of thy Lord, the Inaccessible, the Most High, and quaff thy fill, and be not of them that tarry. I swear by God! The moment thou touchest the Cup with thy lips, the Concourse on high will acclaim thee saying, "Drink with healthy relish, O man that hast truly believed in God!", and the inhabitants of the Cities of Immortality will cry out, "Joy be to thee, O thou that hast drained the Cup of His love!", and the Tongue of Grandeur will hail thee, "Great is the blessedness that awaiteth thee, O My servant, for thou hast attained unto that which none hath attained, except such as have detached themselves from all that is in the heavens and all that is on the earth, and who are the emblems of true detachment."

—Bahá'u'lláh

2

Announce unto My servants the advent of the One Who came unto them with the power of truth bearing the name of 'Alí,* Who dawned above the horizon of holiness with the splendours of a cherished glory, and from Whose right hand flowed the crystal streams of the spirit, laying bare the wonders of a hidden knowledge.

"O people!" He declared, "The clouds of wisdom have been lifted and God hath revealed His Cause. This is that which ye were promised in all the Scriptures. Fear ye God and hasten unto Me. I am, O people, a scion of your Prophet. I have brought unto you verses that bewilder the minds of them that perceive, and this is but a token of God's proof and testimony. Deny them not at the prompting of your idle fancies, and be fair in your judgement. They verily proceed from the religion of God that hath been sent down unto you through the power of truth, would that ye might believe!

"I swear by God, O people! I wish only to rid your religions of all that hath in this day become the cause of contention. These verses, O people, are the breezes of the spirit that are wafting over you and would transmute your mortal condition into eternal life, could ye but fix your gaze upon them. O

---

* The Báb.

45

people! The tree of knowledge hath yielded its fruit upon this everlasting Lote-Tree; the Primal Point hath been unfolded; and the Word of God, the Help in Peril, the Self-Subsisting, hath been fulfilled. O people! The beauty of His countenance hath been revealed, the veils have been parted, the Nightingale hath warbled its melody, the Mount of holiness hath been made resplendent, and all who are in the heavens and on the earth have been illumined, could ye but see with the eye of the spirit!"

But the people made reply, saying: "We deem Thee a speaker of falsehood; nor do we discern in Thine acts that which we had been promised in the books of our forefathers. Never would we follow Thee, even wert Thou to produce for us all the signs of the world."

"O concourse of men!" He declared, "Fear ye God and consider that which He hath ordained to be His immutable proof and abiding testimony unto all that dwell in the heavens and on the earth, did ye but know it. O people! The truth of all that ye have been awaiting, and all that ye have heard from your forefathers and your divines, is established only through these verses. And these, verily, are the verses of holiness that have been vouchsafed unto all who are in the heavens and on the earth, even as ye yourselves can behold.

"If ye believe not in these verses, how then can ye be assured of the truth of your own religion in this day or establish it in the eyes of others? The day is fast approaching when the world and all that it containeth will have perished, and when ye shall stand in the holy court of His presence. Take heed, O people, lest ye be swayed by the elaborate pronouncements of your divines or misconceive the truth of the matter. Hearken unto My counsels and repudiate not the exhortations of God."

The more He extolled the remembrance of God, the greater they waxed in their oppression, until all the divines pronounced sentence against Him, save those that were acquainted with the precepts of God, the All-Glorious, the Best-Beloved. Matters came to such a pass that they united to put Him to death. They suspended Him in the air, and the hosts of misbelief flung at Him the bullets of malice and hatred, piercing the body of the One unto Whom the Holy Spirit is a humble servant, the dust of Whose feet is the object of adoration of the Concourse on high, and from Whose very sandals the inmates of Paradise seek a blessing. Whereupon the inhabitants of the unseen realm wept sore beneath the pavilion of eternity, the pillars of the Throne trembled, the inmost realities of all things were stirred into commotion, and the divine Tree received its full measure of His gleaming blood which was shed upon the earth.

Erelong will God reveal the mystery of this Tree, make it to flourish through the power of truth, and cause it to intone: "Verily I am God, there is none other God but Him. All are My servants whom We have created to carry out My bidding, and by My bidding they all, verily, abide."

This, in truth, is that which We pledged Ourself aforetime to accomplish: to show favour unto those who were brought low in the land and to humble them that have waxed proud. At no time did We send an Apostle, a Prophet, or a Vicegerent whom these wicked souls did not oppose, even as ye witness how these workers of iniquity are raising objections in this day.

Nor have the people ever rejected the truth except after their divines rejected it, and swelled with pride before God, and sought to dispute His verses. Thus did the rejection of the leaders give rise to the rejection of those who followed them in their selfish desires. None among these divines ever bore allegiance unto the new Revelation, save for those who could gaze with the eye of holiness, whose hearts God had tested and proved true for His recognition, to whom He hath given to drink from that chalice of holiness sealed with the musk of the spirit, and who were intoxicated by the wine of certitude which they had quaffed from that chalice. These, verily, are they whom the angels of Paradise will glorify in the garden of eternity and who will delight at every moment in a joy and gladness born of God.

No Prophet have We ever raised up except that He was repudiated by the divines whilst they prided themselves in their learning, even as they do in this day. Say: O concourse of divines! Do ye worship the Calf and abandon the One Who hath created you and taught you that which ye knew not?

O people of the earth! Ponder the state of these workers of iniquity, what they have wrought in the past, and what they pursue in this day. Say: If He Who hath come unto you with clear verses be not the True One from God, even as ye proclaim this day from your seats of worldly honour, then by what proof can ye establish the truth of Muḥammad, Whom we sent aforetime? Be fair in your judgement, O concourse of ill-wishers!

—Bahá'u'lláh

3

Would that thou wert standing at this moment before the Throne and couldst hear how the melodies of eternity issue from the Temple of Bahá! By the one true God, should His creatures but cleanse their ears, and should they hear but a single strain of these melodies, they would, one and all, fall thunderstruck upon the dust in the presence of thy Lord, the All-Glorious, the Most Bountiful. Since, however, they have contended with God, He hath denied them the wonders of His grace and hath reckoned them in His sight as discarded lumps of clay. By God! Wert thou to consider their words, thou wouldst hear what was never heard from the Jews when We sent the Spirit unto them with a perspicuous Book, nor from the concourse of the Gospel when We caused the Day-Star of eternity to dawn above the horizon of Mecca with world-illumining splendours, nor yet from the people of the Qur'án when the heavens of divine knowledge were cleft asunder and God manifested Himself, with the power of the truth and in the shadow of His All-Merciful Name, in the beauty of 'Alí.*

At the mention of this blessed, this hallowed, this exalted and unapproachably wondrous Name, a Name in truth most wondrous, there arise within Me two conditions. I see My

---

* The Báb.

49

heart burning with the fire of grief over that which befell the Beauty of the All-Merciful at the hands of the people of the Qur'án. It is as though every limb of My body were being devoured by a consuming flame that, if left unchecked, would set ablaze the entire world. To this, God Himself beareth Me witness. Likewise I behold tears flowing from Mine eyes, and My limbs, and even the hairs of My head, at the calamities that were visited upon Him by the wicked, who slew God and recognized Him not, and who, boasting of allegiance to but one of His Names, suspended Him in the air and riddled His breast with the bullets of hatred.

Would that the universe had never been called into existence! Would that the world had never been brought into being! Would that no Prophet had ever been raised up, no Messenger sent forth, and no Cause established amongst men! Would that the Name of God had never been manifested betwixt earth and heaven, and that no Books, Tablets, or Scriptures had ever been revealed! Would that the Ancient Beauty had never been made to dwell among these workers of iniquity, nor to suffer at the hands of those who openly disbelieved in God and who committed against Him that which none on earth had ever dared commit! By the one true God! Wert thou, O 'Alí,* to examine My limbs and members, My heart and vitals, thou wouldst discover the traces of those same bullets that struck that Temple of God. Alas, alas! Thus was the Revealer of verses prevented from revealing them, and this Ocean from surging, and this Tree from bearing fruit, and this Cloud from pouring down its rain, and this Sun from

---

* The Súriy-i-Aḥzán was revealed for Mírzá 'Alíy-i-Sayyáh-i-Marághih'í.

giving its light, and this Heaven from ascending on high. Yet, so hath it been irrevocably decreed in this Day.

Would that I had never been, and that My mother had never borne Me! Would that I had never heard of that which befell Him at the hands of those who worshipped the Names of God and yet slew Him Who is their Author, their Creator, their Fashioner, and their Revealer! Woe betide them for following the promptings of self and passion, and for committing that which caused the Maids of Heaven to faint away in their celestial chambers and the Spirit to cover its face in the dust by reason of that which these wolves have inflicted upon the Lord of Lords. All things weep at the tears I shed for Him; all things lament at the sighs I uttered over Our separation. Such indeed is My sorrow that the melodies of eternity can no longer flow from My lips, nor can the breezes of the spirit waft from My heart. And had I not sought to protect Myself, My body would have been cleft asunder and My life extinguished.

Behold, My former Manifestation weepeth in turn and addresseth thee, saying, "O 'Alí! By the righteousness of the one true God! Wert thou to examine My heart, My limbs, and My members, and to observe Mine inner and outer being, thou wouldst find the traces of the darts of rancour that have struck My latter Manifestation Who appeareth in My Name, the All-Glorious! Thus do I lament, and the Concourse on high lament My weeping. Thus do I bewail, and the dwellers of the Tabernacle of names bewail My cries. Thus do I sigh in anguish, and the inhabitants of the cities of eternity shed tears at My sighing for this Wronged One Who findeth Himself among the people of the Bayán. By God, they have inflicted upon Him that which the followers of the Qur'án never inflicted upon Me. Alas for what hath befallen Him at their hands! Whereupon did the denizens of earth and heaven fall distraught upon the dust at that which had afflicted that

Beauty Who was seated upon the throne of divine nearness. Woe to them and to what their hands have wrought every morn and eve!"

Behold, the Ancient Beauty crieth out: "O Pen of the Most High! Turn aside from this theme which hath saddened all that wear the garment of existence, and make mention of another out of mercy for the Concourse on high. By the one true God! His Throne hath well-nigh been overwhelmed, notwithstanding its grandeur and loftiness."

When We heard this call, We ceased Our account of these sorrows and returned to Our previous theme, that thou mayest be fully apprised thereof. O 'Alí, be not dismayed at that which we have recounted to thee of the calamities that have been visited upon Our former and latter Manifestations. Gird up thy loins to assist the Cause of God, and arise in this path with constancy and unbending resolve.

—Bahá'u'lláh

4

A fast ebbing life, so crowded with the accumulated anxieties, disappointments, treacheries and sorrows of a tragic ministry, now moved swiftly towards its climax. The most turbulent period of the Heroic Age of the new Dispensation was rapidly attaining its culmination. The cup of bitter woes which the Herald of that Dispensation had tasted was now full to overflowing. Indeed, He Himself had already foreshadowed His own approaching death. In the Kitáb-i-Panj-Sha'n, one of His last works, He had alluded to the fact that the sixth Naw-Rúz after the declaration of His mission would be the last He was destined to celebrate on earth. In His interpretation of the letter Há, He had voiced His craving for martyrdom, while in the Qayyúmu'l-Asmá' He had actually prophesied the inevitability of such a consummation of His glorious career. Forty days before His final departure from Chihríq He had even collected all the documents in His possession, and placed them, together with His pen-case, His seals and His rings, in the hands of Mullá Báqir, a Letter of the Living, whom He instructed to entrust them to Mullá Abdu'l-Karím-i-Qazvíní, surnamed Mírzá Aḥmad, who was to deliver them to Bahá'u'lláh in Ṭihrán.

While the convulsions of Mázindarán and Nayríz were pursuing their bloody course the Grand Vizir of Náṣiri'd-Dín Sháh, anxiously pondering the significance of these dire happenings, and apprehensive of their repercussions on his countrymen, his government and his sovereign, was feverishly revolving in his mind that fateful decision which was not only destined to leave its indelible imprint on the fortunes of his country, but was to be fraught with such incalculable consequences for the destinies of the whole of mankind. The repressive measures taken against the followers of the Báb, he was by now fully convinced, had but served to inflame their zeal, steel their resolution and confirm their loyalty to their persecuted Faith. The Báb's isolation and captivity had produced the opposite effect to that which the Amír-Niẓám had confidently anticipated. Gravely perturbed, he bitterly condemned the disastrous leniency of his predecessor, Ḥájí Mírzá Áqásí, which had brought matters to such a pass. A more drastic and still more exemplary punishment, he felt, must now be administered to what he regarded as an abomination of heresy which was polluting the civil and ecclesiastical institutions of the realm. Nothing short, he believed, of the extinction of the life of Him Who was the fountain-head of so odious a doctrine and the driving force behind so dynamic a movement could stem the tide that had wrought such havoc throughout the land.

The siege of Zanján was still in progress when he, dispensing with an explicit order from his sovereign, and acting independently of his counsellors and fellow-ministers, dispatched his order to Prince Ḥamzih Mírzá, the Ḥishmatu'd-Dawlih, the governor of Ádhirbáyján, instructing him to execute the Báb. Fearing lest the infliction of such condign punishment in the capital of the realm would set in motion forces he might be powerless to control, he ordered that his Captive be taken to Tabríz, and there be done to death. Confronted with a flat refusal by the indignant Prince to perform what he regarded as a flagitious crime, the Amír-Niẓám commissioned his own brother, Mírzá Ḥasan Khán, to execute his orders.

The usual formalities designed to secure the necessary authorization from the leading mujtahids of Tabríz were hastily and easily completed. Neither Mullá Muḥammad-i-Mamáqání, however, who had penned the Báb's death-warrant on the very day of His examination in Tabríz, nor Ḥájí Mírzá Báqir, nor Mullá Murtaḍá-Qulí, to whose houses their Victim was ignominiously led by the farrásh-báshí, by order of the Grand Vizir, condescended to meet face to face their dreaded Opponent.

Immediately before and soon after this humiliating treatment meted out to the Báb two highly significant incidents occurred, incidents that cast an illuminating light on the mysterious circumstances surrounding the opening phase of His martyrdom. The farrásh-báshí had abruptly interrupted the last conversation which the Báb was confidentially having in one of the rooms of the barracks with His amanuensis Siyyid Ḥusayn, and was drawing the latter aside, and severely rebuking him, when he was thus addressed by his Prisoner: *"Not until I have said to him all those things that I wish to say can any earthly power silence Me. Though all the world be armed against Me, yet shall it be powerless to deter Me from fulfilling, to the last word, My intention."* To the Christian Sám Khán—the colonel of the Armenian regiment ordered to carry out the execution—who, seized with fear lest his act should provoke the wrath of God, had begged to be released from the duty imposed upon him, the Báb gave the following assurance: *"Follow your instructions, and if your intention be sincere, the Almighty is surely able to relieve you of your perplexity."*

Sám Khán accordingly set out to discharge his duty. A spike was driven into a pillar which separated two rooms of the barracks facing the square. Two ropes were fastened to it from which the Báb and one of his disciples, the youthful and devout Mírzá Muḥammad-'Alí-i-Zunúzí, surnamed Anís, who had previously flung himself at the feet of his Master and implored that under no circumstances he be sent away from Him, were separately suspended. The firing squad ranged itself in three files, each of two hundred and fifty men. Each file in turn opened fire until the whole detachment had discharged its bullets. So dense was the smoke from the seven hundred and fifty rifles that the sky was darkened. As soon as the smoke had cleared away the astounded multitude of about ten thousand souls, who had crowded onto the roof of the barracks, as well as the tops of the adjoining houses, beheld a scene which their eyes could scarcely believe.

The Báb had vanished from their sight! Only his companion remained, alive and unscathed, standing beside the wall on which they had been suspended. The ropes by which they had been hung alone were severed. "The Siyyid-i-Báb has gone from our sight!" cried out the bewildered spectators. A frenzied search immediately ensued. He was found, unhurt and unruffled, in the very room He had occupied the night before, engaged in completing His interrupted conversation with His amanuensis. *"I have finished My conversation with Siyyid Ḥusayn"* were the words with which the Prisoner, so providentially preserved, greeted the appearance of the farrásh-báshí, *"Now you may proceed to fulfill your intention."* Recalling the bold assertion his Prisoner had previously made, and shaken by so stunning a revelation, the farrásh-báshí quitted instantly the scene, and resigned his post.

Sám Khán, likewise, remembering, with feelings of awe and wonder, the reassuring words addressed to him by the Báb, ordered his men to leave the barracks immediately, and swore, as he left the courtyard, never again, even at the cost of his life, to repeat that act. Áqá Ján-i-Khamsih, colonel of the body-guard, volunteered to replace him. On the same wall and in the same manner the Báb and His companion were again suspended, while the new regiment formed in line and opened fire upon them. This time, however, their breasts were riddled with bullets, and their bodies completely dissected, with the exception of their faces which were but little marred. *"O wayward generation!"* were the last words of the Báb to the gazing multitude, as the regiment prepared to fire its volley, *"Had you believed in Me every one of you would have followed the example of this youth, who stood in rank above most of you, and would have willingly sacrificed himself in My path. The day will come when you will have recognized Me; that day I shall have ceased to be with you."*

Nor was this all. The very moment the shots were fired a gale of exceptional violence arose and swept over the city. From noon till night a whirlwind of dust obscured the light of the sun, and blinded the eyes of the people. In Shíráz an "earthquake," foreshadowed in no less weighty a Book than the Revelation of St. John, occurred in 1268 A.H. which threw the whole city into turmoil and wrought havoc amongst its people, a havoc that was greatly aggravated by the outbreak of cholera, by famine and other afflictions. In that same year no less than two hundred and fifty of the firing squad, that had replaced Sám Khán's regiment, met their death, together with their officers, in a terrible earthquake, while the remaining five hundred suffered, three years later, as a punishment for their mutiny, the same fate as that which their hands had inflicted upon the Báb. To insure that none of them had survived, they were riddled with a second volley, after which their bodies, pierced with spears and lances, were exposed to the gaze of the people of Tabríz. The prime instigator of the Báb's death, the implacable Amír-Niẓám, together with his brother, his chief accomplice, met their death within two years of that savage act.

On the evening of the very day of the Báb's execution, which fell on the ninth of July 1850 (28th of Sha'bán 1266 A.H.), during the thirty-first year of His age and the seventh of His ministry, the mangled bodies were transferred from the courtyard of the barracks to the edge of the moat outside the gate of the city. Four companies, each consisting of ten sentinels, were ordered to keep watch in turn over them. On the following morning the Russian Consul in Tabríz visited the spot, and ordered the artist who had accompanied him to make a drawing of the remains as they lay beside the moat. In the middle of the following night a follower of the Báb, Ḥájí Sulaymán Khán, succeeded, through the instrumentality of a certain Ḥájí Alláh-Yár, in removing the bodies to the silk factory owned by one of the believers of Mílán, and laid them, the next day, in a specially made wooden casket, which he later transferred to a place of safety. Meanwhile the mullás were boastfully proclaiming from the pulpits that, whereas the holy body of the Immaculate Imám would be preserved from beasts of prey and from all creeping things, this man's body had been devoured by wild animals. No sooner had the news of the transfer of the remains of the Báb and of His fellow-sufferer been communicated to Bahá'u'lláh than He ordered that same Sulaymán Khán to bring them to Ṭihrán, where they were taken to the Imám-Zádih-Ḥasan, from whence they were removed to different places, until the time when, in pursuance of 'Abdu'l-Bahá's instructions, they were transferred to the Holy Land, and were permanently and ceremoniously laid to rest by Him in a specially erected mausoleum on the slopes of Mt. Carmel.

Thus ended a life which posterity will recognize as standing at the confluence of two universal prophetic cycles, the Adamic Cycle stretching back as far as the first dawnings of the world's recorded religious history and the Bahá'í Cycle destined to propel itself across the unborn reaches of time for a period of no less than five thousand centuries. The apotheosis in which such a life attained its consummation marks, as already observed, the culmination of the most heroic phase of the Heroic Age of the Bahá'í Dispensation. It can, moreover, be regarded in no other light except as the most dramatic, the most tragic event transpiring within the entire range of the first Bahá'í century. Indeed it can be rightly acclaimed as unparalleled in the annals of the lives of all the Founders of the world's existing religious systems.

—Shoghi Effendi

5

Moved to share with assembled representatives of American Bahá'í Community gathered beneath the dome of the Most Holy House of Worship in the Bahá'í world, feelings of profound emotion evoked by this historic occasion of the world-wide commemoration of the First Centenary of the Martyrdom of the Blessed Báb, Prophet and Herald of the Faith of Bahá'u'lláh, Founder of the Dispensation marking the culmination of the six thousand year old Adamic Cycle, Inaugurator of the five thousand century Bahá'í Cycle.

Poignantly call to mind the circumstances attending the last act consummating the tragic ministry of the Master-Hero of the most sublime drama in the religious annals of mankind, signalizing the most dramatic event of the most turbulent period of the Heroic Age of the Bahá'í Dispensation, destined to be recognized by posterity as the most precious, momentous sacrifice in the world's spiritual history. Recall the peerless tributes paid to His memory by the Founder of the Faith, acclaiming Him Monarch of God's Messengers, the Primal Point round Whom the realities of all the Prophets circle in adoration. Profoundly stirred by the memory of the agonies He suffered, the glad-tidings He announced, the warnings He uttered, the forces He set in motion, the adversaries He converted, the disciples He raised up, the conflagrations He precipitated, the legacy He left of faith and courage, the love He inspired. Acknowledge with bowed head, joyous, thankful heart the successive, marvelous evidence of His triumphant power in the course of the hundred years elapsed since the last crowning act of His meteoric ministry.

The creative energies released at the hour of the birth of His Revelation, endowing mankind with the potentialities of the attainment of maturity are deranging, during the present transitional age, the equilibrium of the entire planet as the inevitable prelude to the consummation in world unity of the coming of age of the human race. The portentous but unheeded warnings addressed to kings, princes, ecclesiastics are responsible for the successive overthrow of fourteen monarchies of East and West, the collapse of the institution of the Caliphate, the virtual extinction of the Pope's temporal sovereignty, the progressive decline in the fortunes of the ecclesiastical hierarchies of the Islamic, Christian, Jewish, Zoroastrian, and Hindu Faiths.

The Order eulogized and announced in His writings, whose laws Bahá'u'lláh subsequently revealed in the Most Holy Book, whose features 'Abdu'l-Bahá delineated in His Testament, is now passing through its embryonic stage through the emergence of the initial institutions of the world Administrative Order in the five continents of the globe. The clarion call sounded in the Qayyúmu'l-Asmá', summoning the peoples of the West to forsake their homes and proclaim His message, was nobly answered by the communities of the Western Hemisphere headed by the valorous, stalwart American believers, the chosen vanguard of the all-conquering, irresistibly marching army of the Faith in the western world.

The embryonic Faith, maturing three years after His martyrdom, traversing the period of infancy in the course of the Heroic Age of the Faith is now steadily progressing towards maturity in the present Formative Age, destined to attain full stature in the Golden Age of the Bahá'í Dispensation.

Lastly the Holy Seed of infinite preciousness, holding within itself incalculable potentialities representing the culmination of the centuries-old process of the evolution of humanity through the energies released by the series of progressive Revelations starting with Adam and concluded by the Revelation of the Seal of the Prophets, marked by the successive appearance of the branches, leaves, buds, blossoms and plucked, after six brief years by the hand of destiny, ground in the mill of martyrdom and oppression but yielding the oil whose first flickering light cast upon the somber, subterranean walls of the Síyáh-Chál of Ṭihrán, whose fire gathered brilliance in Baghdad and shone in full resplendency in its crystal globe in Adrianople, whose rays warmed and illuminated the fringes of the American, European, Australian continents through the tender ministerings of the Center of the Covenant, whose radiance is now overspreading the surface of the globe during the present Formative Age, whose full splendor is destined in the course of future milleniums to suffuse the entire planet.

—Shoghi Effendi

Station

1

Magnify Thou, O Lord my God, Him Who is the Primal Point, the Divine Mystery, the Unseen Essence, the Dayspring of Divinity, and the Manifestation of Thy Lordship, through Whom all the knowledge of the past and all the knowledge of the future were made plain, through Whom the pearls of Thy hidden wisdom were uncovered, and the mystery of Thy treasured name disclosed, Whom Thou hast appointed as the Announcer of the One through Whose name the letter B and the letter E have been joined and united, through Whom Thy majesty, Thy sovereignty and Thy might were made known, through Whom Thy words have been sent down, and Thy laws set forth with clearness, and Thy signs spread abroad, and Thy Word established, through Whom the hearts of Thy chosen ones were laid bare, and all that were in the heavens and all that were on the earth were gathered together, Whom Thou hast called 'Alí-Muḥammad in the kingdom of Thy names, and the Spirit of Spirits in the Tablets of Thine irrevocable decree, Whom Thou hast invested with Thine own title, unto Whose name all other names have, at Thy bidding and through the power of Thy might, been made to return, and in Whom Thou hast caused all Thine attributes and titles to attain their final consummation. To Him also belong such names as lay hid within Thy stainless tabernacles, in Thine invisible world and Thy sanctified cities.

—Bahá'u'lláh

2

O Ahmad! Bear thou witness that verily He is God and there is no God but Him, the King, the Protector, the Incomparable, the Omnipotent. And that the One Whom He hath sent forth by the name of 'Alí was the true One from God, to Whose commands we are all conforming.

Say: O people be obedient to the ordinances of God, which have been enjoined in the Bayán by the Glorious, the Wise One. Verily He is the King of the Messengers and His book is the Mother Book did ye but know.

—Bahá'u'lláh

3

I am, I am, I am the Promised One! I am the One Whose name you have for a thousand years invoked, at Whose mention you have risen, Whose advent you have longed to witness, and the hour of Whose Revelation you have prayed God to hasten. Verily, I say, it is incumbent upon the peoples of both the East and the West to obey My word, and to pledge allegiance to My person.

—The Báb

4

The substance wherewith God hath created Me is not the clay out of which others have been formed. He hath conferred upon Me that which the worldly-wise can never comprehend, nor the faithful discover. . . . I am one of the sustaining pillars of the Primal Word of God. Whosoever hath recognized Me, hath known all that is true and right, and hath attained all that is good and seemly; and whosoever hath failed to recognize Me, hath turned away from all that is true and right and hath succumbed to everything evil and unseemly.

I swear by the righteousness of Thy Lord, the Lord of all created things, the Lord of all the worlds! Were a man to rear in this world as many edifices as possible and worship God through every virtuous deed which God's knowledge embraceth, and attain the presence of the Lord, and were he, even to a measure less than that which is accountable before God, to bear in his heart a trace of malice towards Me, all his deeds would be reduced to naught and he would be deprived of the glances of God's favor, become the object of His wrath and assuredly perish. For God hath ordained that all the good things which lie in the treasury of His knowledge shall be attained through obedience unto Me, and every fire recorded in His Book, through disobedience unto Me. Methinks in this day and from this station I behold all those who cherish My love and follow My behest abiding within the mansions of

Paradise, and the entire company of Mine adversaries consigned to the lowest depths of hell-fire.

By My life! But for the obligation to acknowledge the Cause of Him Who is the Testimony of God . . . I would not have announced this unto thee. . . . All the keys of heaven God hath chosen to place on My right hand, and all the keys of hell on My left. . . .

I am the Primal Point from which have been generated all created things. I am the Countenance of God Whose splendor can never be obscured, the Light of God Whose radiance can never fade. Whoso recognizeth Me, assurance and all good are in store for him, and whoso faileth to recognize Me, infernal fire and all evil await him. . . .

I swear by God, the Peerless, the Incomparable, the True One: for no other reason hath He—the supreme Testimony of God—invested Me with clear signs and tokens than that all men may be enabled to submit to His Cause.

By the righteousness of Him Who is the Absolute Truth, were the veil to be lifted, thou wouldst witness on this earthly plane all men sorely afflicted with the fire of the wrath of God, a fire fiercer and greater than the fire of hell, with the exception of those who have sought shelter beneath the shade of the tree of My love. For they in very truth are the blissful.
. .

God beareth Me witness, I was not a man of learning, for I was trained as a merchant. In the year sixty* God graciously infused my soul with the conclusive evidences and weighty knowledge which characterize Him Who is the Testimony of God—may peace be upon Him—until finally in that year I

---

* 1260 A.H. (1844 A.D.)

proclaimed God's hidden Cause and unveiled its well-guarded Pillar, in such wise that no one could refute it.

—The Báb

5

In the year one thousand two hundred and sixty [A.H.], when He was in His twenty-fifth year, certain signs became apparent in His conduct, behavior, manners, and demeanor whereby it became evident in Shíráz that He had some conflict in His mind and some other flight beneath His wing. He began to speak and to declare the rank of Báb-hood. Now what He intended by the term *Báb* [Gate] was this, that He was the channel of grace from some great Person still behind the veil of glory, Who was the possessor of countless and boundless perfections, by Whose will He moved, and to the bond of Whose love He clung. And in the first book which He wrote in explanation of the Súrih of Joseph, He addressed Himself in all passages to that Person unseen from Whom He received help and grace, sought for aid in the arrangement of His preliminaries, and craved the sacrifice of life in the way of His love.

—'Abdu'l-Bahá

6

Dearly-beloved friends! That the Báb, the inaugurator of the Bábí Dispensation, is fully entitled to rank as one of the self-sufficient Manifestations of God, that He has been invested with sovereign power and authority, and exercises all the rights and prerogatives of independent Prophethood, is yet another fundamental verity which the Message of Bahá'u'lláh insistently proclaims and which its followers must uncompromisingly uphold. That He is not to be regarded merely as an inspired Precursor of the Bahá'í Revelation, that in His person, as He Himself bears witness in the Persian Bayán, the object of all the Prophets gone before Him has been fulfilled, is a truth which I feel it my duty to demonstrate and emphasize. We would assuredly be failing in our duty to the Faith we profess and would be violating one of its basic and sacred principles if in our words or by our conduct we hesitate to recognize the implications of this root principle of Bahá'í belief, or refuse to uphold unreservedly its integrity and demonstrate its truth. Indeed the chief motive actuating me to undertake the task of editing and translating Nabíl's immortal Narrative has been to enable every follower of the Faith in the West to better understand and more readily grasp the tremendous implications of His exalted station and to more ardently admire and love Him.

There can be no doubt that the claim to the twofold station ordained for the Báb by the Almighty, a claim which He Himself has so boldly advanced, which Bahá'u'lláh has repeatedly affirmed, and to which the Will and Testament of 'Abdu'l-Bahá has finally given the sanction of its testimony, constitutes the most distinctive feature of the Bahá'í Dispensation. It is a further evidence of its uniqueness, a tremendous accession to the strength, to the mysterious power and authority with which this holy cycle has been invested. Indeed the greatness of the Báb consists primarily, not in His being the divinely-appointed Forerunner of so transcendent a Revelation, but rather in His having been invested with the powers inherent in the inaugurator of a separate religious Dispensation, and in His wielding, to a degree unrivaled by the Messengers gone before Him, the scepter of independent Prophethood.

The short duration of His Dispensation, the restricted range within which His laws and ordinances have been made to operate, supply no criterion whatever wherewith to judge its Divine origin and to evaluate the potency of its message. *"That so brief a span,"* Bahá'u'lláh Himself explains, *"should have separated this most mighty and wondrous Revelation from Mine own previous Manifestation, is a secret that no man can unravel and a mystery such as no mind can fathom. Its duration had been foreordained, and no man shall ever discover its reason unless and until he be informed of the contents of My Hidden Book."* "Behold," Bahá'u'lláh further explains in the Kitáb-i-Badí', one of His works refuting the arguments of the people of the Bayán, *"behold, how immediately upon the completion of the ninth year of this wondrous, this most holy and merciful Dispensation, the requisite number of pure, of wholly consecrated and sanctified souls had been most secretly consummated."*

The marvelous happenings that have heralded the advent of the Founder of the Bábí Dispensation, the dramatic circumstances of His own eventful life, the miraculous tragedy of His martyrdom, the magic of His influence exerted on the most eminent and powerful among His countrymen, to all of which every chapter of Nabíl's stirring narrative testifies, should in themselves be regarded as sufficient evidence of the validity of His claim to so exalted a station among the Prophets.

However graphic the record which the eminent chronicler of His life has transmitted to posterity, so luminous a narrative must pale before the glowing tribute paid to the Báb by the pen of Bahá'u'lláh. This tribute the Báb Himself has, by the clear assertion of His claim, abundantly supported, while the written testimonies of 'Abdu'l-Bahá have powerfully reinforced its character and elucidated its meaning.

Where else if not in the Kitáb-i-Íqán can the student of the Bábí Dispensation seek to find those affirmations that unmistakably attest the power and spirit which no man, except he be a Manifestation of God, can manifest? *"Could such a thing,"* exclaims Bahá'u'lláh, *"be made manifest except through the power of a Divine Revelation and the potency of God's invincible Will? By the righteousness of God! Were any one to entertain so great a Revelation in his heart the thought of such a declaration would alone confound him! Were the hearts of all men to be crowded into his heart, he would still hesitate to venture upon so awful an enterprise."* *"No eye,"* He in another passage affirms, *"hath beheld so great an outpouring of bounty, nor hath any ear heard of such a Revelation of loving-kindness . . . The Prophets 'endowed with constancy,' whose loftiness and glory shine as the sun, were each honored with a Book which all have seen, and the verses of which have been duly ascertained. Whereas the verses which have rained from this Cloud of divine mercy have been so abundant that none hath yet been able to estimate their number . . . How can they belittle this Revelation? Hath any age witnessed such momentous happenings?"*

Commenting on the character and influence of those heroes and martyrs whom the spirit of the Báb had so magically transformed Bahá'u'lláh reveals the following: *"If these companions be not the true strivers after God, who else could be called by this name? . . . If these companions, with all their marvelous testimonies and wondrous works, be false, who then is worthy to claim for himself the truth? . . . Has the world since the days of Adam witnessed such tumult, such violent commotion? . . . Methinks, patience was revealed only by virtue of their fortitude, and faithfulness itself was begotten only by their deeds."*

Wishing to stress the sublimity of the Báb's exalted station as compared with that of the Prophets of the past, Bahá'u'lláh in that same epistle asserts: *"No understanding can grasp the nature of His Revelation, nor can any knowledge comprehend the full measure of His Faith."* He then quotes, in confirmation of His argument, these prophetic words: *"Knowledge is twenty and seven letters. All that the Prophets have revealed are two letters thereof. No man thus far hath known more than these two letters. But when the Qá'im shall arise, He will cause the remaining twenty and five letters to be made manifest."* *"Behold,"* He adds, *"how great and lofty is His station! His rank excelleth that of all the Prophets and His Revelation transcendeth the comprehension and understanding of all their chosen ones."* *"Of His Revelation,"* He further adds, *"the Prophets of God, His saints and chosen ones, have either not been informed, or, in pursuance of God's inscrutable decree, they have not disclosed."*

Of all the tributes which Bahá'u'lláh's unerring pen has chosen to pay to the memory of the Báb, His "Best-Beloved," the most memorable and touching is this brief, yet eloquent passage which so greatly enhances the value of the concluding passages of that same epistle. *"Amidst them all,"* He writes, referring to the afflictive trials and dangers besetting Him in the city of Baghdád, *"We stand life in hand wholly resigned to His Will, that perchance through God's loving kindness and grace, this revealed and manifest Letter* (Bahá'u'lláh) *may lay down His life as a sacrifice in the path of the Primal Point, the most exalted Word* (the Báb). *By Him, at Whose bidding the Spirit hath spoken, but for this yearning of Our soul, We would not, for one moment, have tarried any longer in this city."*

Dearly-beloved friends! So resounding a praise, so bold an assertion issued by the pen of Bahá'u'lláh in so weighty a work, are fully re-echoed in the language in which the Source of the Bábí Revelation has chosen to clothe the claims He Himself has advanced. *"I am the Mystic Fane,"* the Báb thus proclaims His station in the Qayyúmu'l-Asmá', *"which the Hand of Omnipotence hath reared. I am the Lamp which the Finger of God hath lit within its niche and caused to shine with deathless splendor. I am the Flame of that supernal Light that glowed upon Sinai in the gladsome Spot, and lay concealed in the midst of the Burning Bush." "O Qurratu'l-'Ayn!"* He, addressing Himself in that same commentary, exclaims, *"I recognize in Thee none other except the 'Great Announcement'—the Announcement voiced by the Concourse on high. By this name, I bear witness, they that circle the Throne of Glory have ever known Thee." "With each and every Prophet, Whom We have sent down in the past,"* He further adds, *"We have established a separate Covenant concerning the 'Remembrance of God' and His Day. Manifest, in the realm of glory and through the power of truth, are the 'Remembrance of God' and His Day before the eyes of the angels that circle His mercy-seat." "Should it be Our wish,"* He again affirms, *"it is in Our power to compel, through the agency of but one letter of Our Revelation, the world and all that is therein to recognize, in less than the twinkling of an eye the truth of Our Cause."*

"*I am the Primal Point,*" the Báb thus addresses Muḥam-mad Sháh from the prison-fortress of Máh-Kú, "*from which have been generated all created things . . . I am the Countenance of God Whose splendor can never be obscured, the light of God whose radiance can never fade . . . All the keys of heaven God hath chosen to place on My right hand, and all the keys of hell on My left . . . I am one of the sustaining pillars of the Primal Word of God. Whosoever hath recognized Me, hath known all that is true and right, and hath attained all that is good and seemly . . . The substance wherewith God hath created Me is not the clay out of which others have been formed. He hath conferred upon Me that which the worldly-wise can never comprehend, nor the faith-ful discover.*" "*Should a tiny ant,*" the Báb, wishing to stress the limitless potentialities latent in His Dispensation, characteris-tically affirms, "*desire in this day to be possessed of such power as to be able to unravel the abstrusest and most bewildering passages of the Qur'án, its wish will no doubt be fulfilled, inasmuch as the mystery of eternal might vibrates within the innermost being of all created things.*" "*If so helpless a creature,*" is 'Abdu'l-Bahá's comment on so startling an affirmation, "*can be endowed with so subtle a capacity, how much more efficacious must be the power released through the liberal effusions of the grace of Bahá'u'lláh!*"

To these authoritative assertions and solemn declarations made by Bahá'u'lláh and the Báb must be added 'Abdu'l-Bahá's own incontrovertible testimony. He, the appointed interpreter of the utterances of both Bahá'u'lláh and the Báb, corroborates, not by implication but in clear and categorical language, both in His Tablets and in His Testament, the truth of the statements to which I have already referred.

In a Tablet addressed to a Bahá'í in Mázindarán, in which He unfolds the meaning of a misinterpreted statement attributed to Him regarding the rise of the Sun of Truth in this century,

He sets forth, briefly but conclusively, what should remain for all time our true conception of the relationship between the two Manifestations associated with the Bahá'í Dispensation. *"In making such a statement,"* He explains, *"I had in mind no one else except the Báb and Bahá'u'lláh, the character of whose Revelations it had been my purpose to elucidate. The Revelation of the Báb may be likened to the sun, its station corresponding to the first sign of the Zodiac—the sign Aries—which the sun enters at the Vernal Equinox. The station of Bahá'u'lláh's Revelation, on the other hand, is represented by the sign Leo, the sun's mid-summer and highest station. By this is meant that this holy Dispensation is illumined with the light of the Sun of Truth shining from its most exalted station, and in the plenitude of its resplendency, its heat and glory."*

"The Báb, the Exalted One," 'Abdu'l-Bahá more specifically affirms in another Tablet, *"is the Morn of Truth, the splendor of Whose light shineth throughout all regions. He is also the Harbinger of the Most Great Light, the Abhá Luminary. The Blessed Beauty is the One promised by the sacred books of the past, the revelation of the Source of light that shone upon Mount Sinai, Whose fire glowed in the midst of the Burning Bush. We are, one and all, servants of their threshold, and stand each as a lowly keeper at their door."* *"Every proof and prophecy,"* is His still more emphatic warning, *"every manner of evidence, whether based on reason or on the text of the scriptures and traditions, are to be regarded as centered in the persons of Bahá'u'lláh and the Báb. In them is to be found their complete fulfillment."*

And finally, in His Will and Testament, the repository of His last wishes and parting instructions, He in the following passage, specifically designed to set forth the guiding principles of Bahá'í belief, sets the seal of His testimony on the Báb's dual and exalted station: *"The foundation of the belief of the people of Bahá (may my life be offered up for them) is this:*

His holiness the exalted One (the Báb) *is the Manifestation of the unity and oneness of God and the Forerunner of the Ancient Beauty* (Bahá'u'lláh). *His holiness, the Abhá Beauty* (Bahá'u'lláh) *(may my life be offered up as a sacrifice for His steadfast friends) is the supreme Manifestation of God and the Dayspring of His most divine Essence."* "*All others,*" He significantly adds, "*are servants unto Him and do His bidding.*"

—Shoghi Effendi

Prayers and Meditations

1

O God, my God, my Beloved, my heart's Desire.

—The Báb

2

Say: God sufficeth all things above all things, and nothing in the heavens or in the earth but God sufficeth. Verily, He is in Himself the Knower, the Sustainer, the Omnipotent.

—The Báb

3

O Lord! Unto Thee I repair for refuge, and toward all Thy signs I set my heart.

O Lord! Whether traveling or at home, and in my occupation or in my work, I place my whole trust in Thee.

Grant me then Thy sufficing help so as to make me independent of all things, O Thou Who art unsurpassed in Thy mercy!

Bestow upon me my portion, O Lord, as Thou pleasest, and cause me to be satisfied with whatsoever Thou hast ordained for me.

Thine is the absolute authority to command.

—The Báb

4

Is there any Remover of difficulties save God? Say: Praised be God! He is God! All are His servants, and all abide by His bidding!

—The Báb

5

Lauded be Thy Name, O Lord our God! Thou art in truth the Knower of things unseen. Ordain for us such good as Thine all-embracing knowledge can measure. Thou art the sovereign Lord, the Almighty, the Best-Beloved.

All praise be unto Thee, O Lord! We shall seek Thy grace on the appointed Day and shall put our whole reliance in Thee, Who art our Lord. Glorified art Thou, O God! Grant us that which is good and seemly that we may be able to dispense with everything but Thee. Verily, Thou art the Lord of all worlds.

O God! Recompense those who endure patiently in Thy days, and strengthen their hearts to walk undeviatingly in the path of Truth. Grant then, O Lord, such goodly gifts as would enable them to gain admittance into Thy blissful Paradise. Exalted art Thou, O Lord God. Let Thy heavenly blessings descend upon homes whose inmates have believed in Thee. Verily, unsurpassed art Thou in sending down divine blessings. Send forth, O God, such hosts as would render Thy faithful servants victorious. Thou dost fashion the created things through the power of Thy decree as Thou pleasest. Thou art in truth the Sovereign, the Creator, the All-Wise.

Say: God is indeed the Maker of all things. He giveth sustenance in plenty to whomsoever He willeth. He is the Creator, the Source of all beings, the Fashioner, the Almighty, the Maker, the All-Wise. He is the Bearer of the most excellent titles throughout the heavens and the earth and whatever lieth between them. All do His bidding, and all the dwellers of earth and heaven celebrate His praise, and unto Him shall all return.

—The Báb

6

O my God, my Lord and my Master! I have detached myself from my kindred and have sought through Thee to become independent of all that dwell on earth and ever ready to receive that which is praiseworthy in Thy sight. Bestow on me such good as will make me independent of aught else but Thee, and grant me an ampler share of Thy boundless favors. Verily, Thou art the Lord of grace abounding.

—The Báb

7

In the Name of thy Lord, the Creator, the Sovereign, the All-Sufficing, the Most Exalted, He Whose help is implored by all men.

Say: O my God! O Thou Who art the Maker of the heavens and of the earth, O Lord of the Kingdom! Thou well knowest the secrets of my heart, while Thy Being is inscrutable to all save Thyself. Thou seest whatsoever is of me, while no one else can do this save Thee. Vouchsafe unto me, through Thy grace, what will enable me to dispense with all except Thee, and destine for me that which will make me independent of everyone else besides Thee. Grant that I may reap the benefit of my life in this world and in the next. Open to my face the portals of Thy grace, and graciously confer upon me Thy tender mercy and bestowals.

O Thou Who art the Lord of grace abounding! Let Thy celestial aid surround those who love Thee, and bestow upon us the gifts and the bounties Thou dost possess. Be Thou sufficient unto us of all things, forgive our sins and have mercy upon us. Thou art our Lord and the Lord of all created things. No one else do we invoke but Thee, and naught do we beseech but Thy favors. Thou art the Lord of bounty and grace, invincible in Thy power and the most skillful in Thy designs. No God is there but Thee, the All-Possessing, the Most Exalted.

Confer Thy blessings, O my Lord, upon the Messengers, the holy ones and the righteous. Verily, Thou art God, the Peerless, the All-Compelling.

—The Báb

8

O God our Lord! Protect us through Thy grace from whatsoever may be repugnant unto Thee, and vouchsafe unto us that which well beseemeth Thee. Give us more out of Thy bounty, and bless us. Pardon us for the things we have done, and wash away our sins, and forgive us with Thy gracious forgiveness. Verily, Thou art the Most Exalted, the Self-Subsisting.

Thy loving providence hath encompassed all created things in the heavens and on the earth, and Thy forgiveness hath surpassed the whole creation. Thine is sovereignty; in Thy hand are the Kingdoms of Creation and Revelation; in Thy right hand Thou holdest all created things, and within Thy grasp are the assigned measures of forgiveness. Thou forgivest whomsoever among Thy servants Thou pleasest. Verily, Thou art the Ever-Forgiving, the All-Loving. Nothing whatsoever escapeth Thy knowledge, and naught is there which is hidden from Thee.

O God our Lord! Protect us through the potency of Thy might, enable us to enter Thy wondrous surging ocean, and grant us that which well befitteth Thee.

Thou art the Sovereign Ruler, the Mighty Doer, the Exalted, the All-Loving.

—The Báb

9

I beg Thee to forgive me, O my Lord, for every mention but the mention of Thee, and for every praise but the praise of Thee, and for every delight but delight in Thy nearness, and for every pleasure but the pleasure of communion with Thee, and for every joy but the joy of Thy love and of Thy good-pleasure, and for all things pertaining unto me which bear no relationship unto Thee, O Thou Who art the Lord of lords, He Who provideth the means and unlocketh the doors.

—The Báb

10

Glory be unto Thee, O God. How can I make mention of Thee while Thou art sanctified from the praise of all mankind. Magnified be Thy Name, O God, Thou art the King, the Eternal Truth; Thou knowest what is in the heavens and on the earth, and unto Thee must all return. Thou hast sent down Thy divinely ordained Revelation according to a clear measure. Praised art Thou, O Lord! At Thy behest Thou dost render victorious whomsoever Thou willest, through the hosts of heaven and earth and whatsoever existeth between them. Thou art the Sovereign, the Eternal Truth, the Lord of invincible might.

Glorified art Thou, O Lord! Thou forgivest at all times the sins of such among Thy servants as implore Thy pardon. Wash away my sins and the sins of those who seek Thy forgiveness at dawn, who pray to Thee in the daytime and in the night season, who yearn after naught save God, who offer up whatsoever God hath graciously bestowed upon them, who celebrate Thy praise at morn and eventide, and who are not remiss in their duties.

—The Báb

11

Verily I am Thy servant, O my God, and Thy poor one and Thy suppliant and Thy wretched creature. I have arrived at Thy gate, seeking Thy shelter. I have found no contentment save in Thy love, no exultation except in Thy remembrance, no eagerness but in obedience to Thee, no joy save in Thy nearness, and no tranquility except in reunion with Thee, notwithstanding that I am conscious that all created things are debarred from Thy sublime Essence and the entire creation is denied access to Thine inmost Being. Whenever I attempt to approach Thee, I perceive nothing in myself but the tokens of Thy grace and behold naught in my being but the revelations of Thy loving-kindness. How can one who is but Thy creature seek reunion with Thee and attain unto Thy presence, whereas no created thing can ever be associated with Thee, nor can aught comprehend Thee? How is it possible for a lowly servant to recognize Thee and to extol Thy praise, notwithstanding that Thou hast destined for him the revelations of Thy dominion and the wondrous testimonies of Thy sovereignty? Thus every created thing beareth witness that it is debarred from the sanctuary of Thy presence by reason of the limitations imposed upon its inner reality. It is undisputed, however, that the influence of Thine attraction hath everlastingly been inherent in the realities of Thy handiwork, although that which beseemeth the hallowed court of Thy providence is exalted beyond the attainment of the entire creation. This indicateth, O my God, my utter powerlessness to praise Thee and revealeth my utmost impotence in yielding thanks unto Thee; and how much more to attain the recognition of Thy divine unity or to succeed in reaching the clear tokens of Thy praise, Thy sanctity and Thy glory. Nay, by Thy might, I yearn for naught but Thine Own Self and seek no one other than Thee.

—The Báb

12

O my God! There is no one but Thee to allay the anguish of my soul, and Thou art my highest aspiration, O my God. My heart is wedded to none save Thee and such as Thou dost love. I solemnly declare that my life and death are both for Thee. Verily Thou art incomparable and hast no partner.

O my Lord! I beg Thee to forgive me for shutting myself out from Thee. By Thy glory and majesty, I have failed to befittingly recognize Thee and to worship Thee, while Thou dost make Thyself known unto me and callest me to remembrance as beseemeth Thy station. Grievous woe would betide me, O my Lord, wert Thou to take hold of me by reason of my misdeeds and trespasses. No helper do I know of other than Thee. No refuge do I have to flee to save Thee. None among Thy creatures can dare to intercede with Thyself without Thy leave. I hold fast to Thy love before Thy court, and, according to Thy bidding, I earnestly pray unto Thee as befitteth Thy glory. I beg Thee to heed my call as Thou hast promised me. Verily Thou art God; no God is there but Thee. Alone and unaided, Thou art independent of all created things. Neither can the devotion of Thy lovers profit Thee, nor the evil doings of the faithless harm Thee. Verily Thou art my God, He Who will never fail in His promise.

O my God! I beseech Thee by the evidences of Thy favor, to let me draw nigh to the sublime heights of Thy holy presence, and protect me from inclining myself toward the subtle allusions of aught else but Thee. Guide my steps, O my God, unto that which is acceptable and pleasing to Thee. Shield me, through Thy might, from the fury of Thy wrath and chastisement, and hold me back from entering habitations not desired by Thee.

—The Báb

13

All majesty and glory, O my God, and all dominion and light and grandeur and splendor be unto Thee. Thou bestowest sovereignty on whom Thou willest and dost withhold it from whom Thou desirest. No God is there but Thee, the All-Possessing, the Most Exalted. Thou art He Who createth from naught the universe and all that dwell therein. There is nothing worthy of Thee except Thyself, while all else but Thee are as outcasts in Thy holy presence and are as nothing when compared to the glory of Thine Own Being.

Far be it from me to extol Thy virtues save by what Thou hast extolled Thyself in Thy weighty Book where Thou sayest, "No vision taketh in Him, but He taketh in all vision. He is the Subtile, the All-Perceiving."* Glory be unto Thee, O my God, indeed no mind or vision, however keen or discriminating, can ever grasp the nature of the most insignificant of Thy signs. Verily, Thou art God, no God is there besides Thee. I bear witness that Thou Thyself alone art the sole expression of Thine attributes, that the praise of no one besides Thee can ever attain to Thy holy court nor can Thine attributes ever be fathomed by anyone other than Thyself.

Glory be unto Thee, Thou art exalted above the description of anyone save Thyself, since it is beyond human concep-

---

* Qur'án 6:103.

tion to befittingly magnify Thy virtues or to comprehend the inmost reality of Thine Essence. Far be it from Thy glory that Thy creatures should describe Thee or that anyone besides Thyself should ever know Thee. I have known Thee, O my God, by reason of Thy making Thyself known unto me, for hadst Thou not revealed Thyself unto me, I would not have known Thee. I worship Thee by virtue of Thy summoning me unto Thee, for had it not been for Thy summons I would not have worshiped Thee.

—The Báb

14

Ordain for me, O my Lord, and for those who believe in Thee that which is deemed best for us in Thine estimation, as set forth in the Mother Book, for within the grasp of Thy hand Thou holdest the determined measures of all things.

Thy goodly gifts are unceasingly showered upon such as cherish Thy love, and the wondrous tokens of Thy heavenly bounties are amply bestowed on those who recognize Thy divine Unity. We commit unto Thy care whatsoever Thou hast destined for us, and implore Thee to grant us all the good that Thy knowledge embraceth.

Protect me, O my Lord, from every evil that Thine omniscience perceiveth, inasmuch as there is no power nor strength but in Thee, no triumph is forthcoming save from Thy presence, and it is Thine alone to command. Whatever God hath willed hath been, and that which He hath not willed shall not be.

There is no power nor strength except in God, the Most Exalted, the Most Mighty.

—The Báb

15

Glory be to Thee, O God! Thou art the God Who hath existed before all things, Who will exist after all things and will last beyond all things. Thou art the God Who knoweth all things, and is supreme over all things. Thou art the God Who dealeth mercifully with all things, Who judgeth between all things and Whose vision embraceth all things. Thou art God my Lord, Thou art aware of my position, Thou dost witness my inner and outer being.

Grant Thy forgiveness unto me and unto the believers who responded to Thy Call. Be Thou my sufficing helper against the mischief of whosoever may desire to inflict sorrow upon me or wish me ill. Verily, Thou art the Lord of all created things. Thou dost suffice everyone, while no one can be self-sufficient without Thee.

—The Báb

16

Vouchsafe unto me, O my God, the full measure of Thy love and Thy good-pleasure, and through the attractions of Thy resplendent light enrapture our hearts, O Thou Who art the Supreme Evidence and the All-Glorified. Send down upon me, as a token of Thy grace, Thy vitalizing breezes, throughout the daytime and in the night season, O Lord of bounty.

No deed have I done, O my God, to merit beholding Thy face, and I know of a certainty that were I to live as long as the world lasts I would fail to accomplish any deed such as to deserve this favor, inasmuch as the station of a servant shall ever fall short of access to Thy holy precincts, unless Thy bounty should reach me and Thy tender mercy pervade me and Thy loving-kindness encompass me.

All praise be unto Thee, O Thou besides Whom there is none other God. Graciously enable me to ascend unto Thee, to be granted the honor of dwelling in Thy nearness and to have communion with Thee alone. No God is there but Thee.

Indeed shouldst Thou desire to confer blessing upon a servant Thou wouldst blot out from the realm of his heart every mention or disposition except Thine Own mention; and shouldst Thou ordain evil for a servant by reason of that which his hands have unjustly wrought before Thy face, Thou wouldst test him with the benefits of this world and of the next that he might become preoccupied therewith and forget Thy remembrance.

—The Báb

17

Praise be to Thee, O Lord, my Best Beloved! Make me steadfast in Thy Cause, and grant that I may be reckoned among those who have not violated Thy Covenant nor followed the gods of their own idle fancy. Enable me, then, to obtain a seat of truth in Thy presence, bestow upon me a token of Thy mercy and let me join with such of Thy servants as shall have no fear nor shall they be put to grief. Abandon me not to myself, O my Lord, nor deprive me of recognizing Him Who is the Manifestation of Thine Own Self, nor account me with such as have turned away from Thy holy presence. Number me, O my God, with those who are privileged to fix their gaze upon Thy Beauty and who take such delight therein that they would not exchange a single moment thereof with the sovereignty of the kingdom of heavens and earth or with the entire realm of creation. Have mercy on me, O Lord, in these days when the peoples of Thine earth have erred grievously; supply me then, O my God, with that which is good and seemly in Thine estimation. Thou art, verily, the All-Powerful, the Gracious, the Bountiful, the Ever-Forgiving.

Grant, O my God, that I may not be reckoned among those whose ears are deaf, whose eyes are blind, whose tongues are speechless and whose hearts have failed to comprehend. Deliver me, O Lord, from the fire of ignorance and of selfish desire, suffer me to be admitted into the precincts of Thy transcendent mercy and send down upon me that which

Thou hast ordained for Thy chosen ones. Potent art Thou to do what Thou willest. Verily, Thou art the Help in Peril, the Self-Subsisting.

—The Báb

18

Praised and glorified art Thou, O God! Grant that the day of attaining Thy holy presence may be fast approaching. Cheer our hearts through the potency of Thy love and good-pleasure, and bestow upon us steadfastness that we may willingly submit to Thy Will and Thy Decree. Verily, Thy knowledge embraceth all the things Thou hast created or wilt create, and Thy celestial might transcendeth whatsoever Thou hast called or wilt call into being. There is none to be worshiped but Thee, there is none to be desired except Thee, there is none to be adored besides Thee and there is naught to be loved save Thy good-pleasure.

Verily, Thou art the supreme Ruler, the Sovereign Truth, the Help in Peril, the Self-Subsisting.

—The Báb

19

I adjure Thee by Thy might, O my God! Let no harm beset me in times of tests, and in moments of heedlessness guide my steps aright through Thine inspiration. Thou art God, potent art Thou to do what Thou desirest. No one can withstand Thy Will or thwart Thy Purpose.

—The Báb

20

O Lord! Thou art the Remover of every anguish and the Dispeller of every affliction. Thou art He Who banisheth every sorrow and setteth free every slave, the Redeemer of every soul. O Lord! Grant deliverance through Thy mercy, and reckon me among such servants of Thine as have gained salvation.

—The Báb

21

O Lord! Enable all the peoples of the earth to gain admittance into the Paradise of Thy Faith, so that no created being may remain beyond the bounds of Thy good-pleasure.

From time immemorial Thou hast been potent to do what pleaseth Thee and transcendent above whatsoever Thou desirest.

—The Báb

22

O Lord! Provide for the speedy growth of the Tree of Thy divine Unity; water it then, O Lord, with the flowing waters of Thy good-pleasure, and cause it, before the revelations of Thy divine assurance, to yield such fruits as Thou desirest for Thy glorification and exaltation, Thy praise and thanksgiving, and to magnify Thy Name, to laud the oneness of Thine Essence and to offer adoration unto Thee, inasmuch as all this lieth within Thy grasp and in that of none other.

Great is the blessedness of those whose blood Thou hast chosen wherewith to water the Tree of Thine affirmation, and thus to exalt Thy holy and immutable Word.

—The Báb

Notes

Introduction

1. Bahá'u'lláh, *Prayers and Meditations by Bahá'u'lláh*, no. 61. For comprehensive accounts of the Ministry of the Báb, see Shoghi Effendi, *God Passes By* [Bahá'í Publishing Trust, 1974] and Nabíl-i-A'ẓam, *The Dawn-Breakers* [Bahá'í Publishing Trust, 1999]. For a more succinct summary, see https://www.bahai.org/the-bab/.

Birth

1. Bahá'u'lláh, *Days of Remembrance*, no. 40.
2. Ibid., no. 41.
3. The Báb, *Selections from the Writings of the Báb*, no. 7:4:2–3.
4. Ibid., no. 7:12:1–2.
5. 'Abdu'l-Bahá, *A Traveler's Narrative*, p. 4.

Declaration

1. Bahá'u'lláh, "Lawḥ-i-Náqús," (Tablet of the Bell), *Days of Remembrance*, no. 26.
2. Ibid., "Lawḥ-i-Ghulámu'l-Khuld," (Tablet of the Immortal Youth), *Days of Remembrance*, no. 27.
3. Ibid., *Days of Remembrance*, no. 28.
4. 'Abdu'l-Bahá, *The Promulgation of Universal Peace*, pp. 196–98.
5. Ibid., *Some Answered Questions*, no. 8.
6. Shoghi Effendi, *God Passes By*, pp. 6–9.

Martyrdom

1. Bahá'u'lláh, *Days of Remembrance*, no. 34.

113

2. Ibid., excerpt from the "Súriy-i-Nuṣḥ," (Súrih of Counsel), *Days of Remembrance*, no. 35.

3. Ibid., excerpt from the "Súriy-i-Aḥzán," (Súrih of Sorrows), *Days of Remembrance*, no. 39.

4. Shoghi Effendi, *God Passes By*, pp. 80–87.

5. Ibid., *Citadel of Faith*, pp. 80–82.

Station

1. Bahá'u'lláh, *Prayers and Meditations by Bahá'u'lláh*, no. 61.

2. Ibid., "The Tablet of Aḥmad," in *Bahá'í Prayers*, p. 302.

3. The Báb, quoted in Shoghi Effendi, *God Passes By*, p. 34.

4. Ibid., *Selections from the Writings of the Báb*, no. 1:4:1–7.

5. 'Abdu'l-Bahá, *A Traveler's Narrative*, p. 4.

6. Shoghi Effendi, "The Dispensation of Bahá'u'lláh," *The World Order of Bahá'u'lláh*, pp. 123–28.

Prayers and Meditations

1. The Báb, in *Bahá'í Prayers*, p. 129.

2. Ibid., p. 55.

3. Ibid., pp. 55–56.

4. Ibid., p. 221.

5. Ibid., pp. 48–49.

6. Ibid., p. 22.

7. Ibid., pp. 53–54.

8. Ibid., pp. 76–77.

9. Ibid., p. 78.

10. Ibid., pp. 78–79.

11. Ibid., pp. 126–28.

12. Ibid., pp. 128–29.

13. Ibid., pp. 139–40.

14. Ibid., pp. 146–47.

15. Ibid., pp. 147–48.

16. Ibid., pp. 170–71.

17. Ibid., pp. 186–87.

18. Ibid., pp. 187–88.

19. Ibid., p. 223.

20. Ibid.

21. Ibid., p. 229.
22. Ibid. pp. 227–28.

Bibliography

Works of Bahá'u'lláh

Days of Remembrance: Selections from the Writings of Bahá'u'lláh for Bahá'í Holy Days. Haifa: Bahá'í World Center, 2016.

Prayers and Meditations by Bahá'u'lláh. Translated by Shoghi Effendi. Wilmette, IL: Bahá'í Publishing Trust, 2013.

Works of the Báb

Selections from the Writings of the Báb. Compiled by the Research Department of the Universal House of Justice. Translated by Habib Taherzadeh et al. Wilmette, IL: Bahá'í Publishing Trust, 2006.

Works of 'Abdu'l-Bahá

The Promulgation of Universal Peace: Talks Delivered by 'Abdu'l-Bahá during His Visit to the United States and Canada in 1912. Compiled by Howard MacNutt. Wilmette, IL: Bahá'í Publishing, 2007.

Some Answered Questions. Translated by a committee of the Universal House of Justice. Pocket-size ed. Wilmette, IL: Bahá'í Publishing Trust, 2014.

A Traveler's Narrative: Written to Illustrate the Episode of the Báb. Translated by Edward G. Browne. Wilmette, IL: Bahá'í Publishing Trust, 1980.

Works of Shoghi Effendi

Citadel of Faith: Messages to America 1947–1957. Wilmette, IL: Bahá'í Publishing Trust, 1965.

God Passes By. New ed. Wilmette, IL: Bahá'í Publishing Trust, 1974.

The World Order of Bahá'u'lláh: Selected Letters. 1st pocket-size ed. Wilmette, IL: Bahá'í Publishing Trust, 1991.

Compilations

Bahá'u'lláh, the Báb, and 'Abdu'l-Bahá. *Bahá'í Prayers: A Selection of Prayers Revealed by Bahá'u'lláh, the Báb, and 'Abdu'l-Bahá.* New ed. Wilmette, IL: Bahá'í Publishing Trust, 2002.

Other Works

Nábil-i-A'ẓam [Muḥammad-i-Zarandí]. *The Dawn-Breakers: Nabíl's Narrative of the Early Days of the Bahá'í Revelation.* Translated and edited by Shoghi Effendi. Wilmette, IL: Bahá'í Publishing Trust, 1999.